Choices
for Later Life

MAKING THE MOST OF LIFE
AFTER 50

MARIE LACHEZE

PIATKUS

Copyright © 2007 by Marie Lacheze

First published in 2007 by
Piatkus Books Limited
5 Windmill Street
London W1T 2JA
e-mail: info@piatkus.co.uk

The moral right of the author has been asserted

A catalogue record for this book is available from the British Library

ISBN 0 7499 2699 6

Text design by Paul Saunders

This book has been printed on paper manufactured with respect for the environment using wood from managed sustainable resources

Typeset by Phoenix Photosetting, Chatham, Kent ·
www.phoenixphotosetting.co.uk
Printed and bound in Great Britain by
Antony Rowe Ltd, Chippenham, Wiltshire

Contents

Part 4: *Our Money*

To all of you who hope
for fulfilling days to the very end.

Acknowledgements

···

M Y THANKS TO ALL of you who took me into your confidence and talked to me or completed my questionnaire, both at home and abroad. This book is based in great part on your experience and I appreciate the time and effort you spent in bringing your thoughts together and offering suggestions. Thanks also to all the doctors, nurses, carers, therapists and all the others who gave me their professional views and comments.

Many of you will recognise yourselves in this book although all names and some of the circumstances have been changed to avoid embarrassment. Special thanks to Thecla Schreuders for her ongoing encouragement and for the order and clarity she brought to the manuscript. Her professional advice as producer and writer has been invaluable. Thank you too, of course, to my husband whose insight and advice over many years have helped so much to make our choices easier, and to all the family for their patience and continuing support.

Introduction

···

How this book came to be written

When I approached retirement, I thought I would seek out some advice on the best way to approach the next 20 years or so of my life. But few of my friends or acquaintances had much to say on the matter, and the recommendations I did get were very general such as 'make sure you have lots of interests' or 'you'll have time to do all the things you couldn't do before' or 'you'll need to have a project'. The published material wasn't very helpful either, dealing mainly with health and finance or resources for the very elderly who need care. Often the tone was simplistic, 'If you're bored, be versatile, make a wish list of all the things you want to do and go out with a friend and do them!'[1] recounting tales of happy retirees who had retrained to become plastic surgeons or set up a successful greeting card business in their seventies. Frequently I couldn't relate to the assumptions being made: that I wanted to remain 'young', that I had a wide network of friends and family nearby to offer support, or that I had unlimited access to activities and services.

I then turned to professionals who deal every day with those in later life: the carers, psychologists, doctors and social workers, but was disappointed by the lack of awareness behind their response. Invariably their message was: 'It is up to each individual to find his or her own lifestyle. If you don't have a positive outlook on life there isn't much we can do. Each person is so different there is no advice that is universally applicable.'

I had reached a point of real frustration, when someone said to me, 'If you can't find what you want, why don't you write a book for people like us?' and so I set about doing just that.

Having read as much as I could and talked to a great many focus groups, I distributed 100 questionnaires to people aged between 50 and 80, asking them for their advice, opinions and experiences of later life. It is their responses that form the backbone of this book. They confirmed my conviction that people's expectations and experience of later years have much in common, but when faced with important choices at this time appropriate help is not always available.

So I felt comforted in the thought that there was indeed a common experience that could be discussed and, although the names have been changed, I quote extensively from these questionnaires and personal interviews throughout this book.

The form of this book

The book is divided into four parts: Our Bodies, Our Minds, Our World and Our Money, and I discuss those issues most frequently mentioned by those who took part and where the choices to be made were often the most complex. Having discussed these issues, including some examples, I then follow up with some 'first steps' and suggestions on how to approach the issues 'differently'. Some of the options set out *are* contradictory, but each of you will make the choice you feel most comfortable with.

Throughout this book I have tried to avoid guilt-inducing words or phrases such as 'have to', 'must' and 'should', which I myself find very discouraging, and I do not assume that our choices are endless. We have some, of course, and those are the ones I have written about, but I am very aware that many of us have alternative lifestyles, financial or physical constraints or live in communities confined by geographical or psychological boundaries that limit the available options. The only assumptions I have made in this book are that you, the reader are interested in the opinions and suggestions of others, and also that you do have some disposable income and some physical autonomy, however limited.

I am in my sixties and live in a very conservative rural area. I have had to face many of the situations which inevitably crop up in later life whether dealing with very elderly parents or trying to keep fit. With scattered friends and a family ranging in age from three to 95, I have had to make some difficult choices, but my experience seems to mirror closely that of those of you who have contributed to this book.

In considering many of the questions raised, my professional experience as a management consultant has helped me to present choices here which even the reluctant and ill-equipped can relate to. They concentrate on the practical, applicable and realistic, avoiding value judgements and theory.

This book is a contribution to the debate, providing a sense of direction rather than specifying a particular path to be followed. My sincere hope is that you will find some points in this book which are relevant to your life and find the suggestions helpful.

Who we are – how we see ourselves

'We' are those who are approaching or who are in retirement, a generation especially blessed as the number of healthy active years we can expect to live increases in leaps and bounds. Unlike the generations that follow us, most of us do not face problems of reduced pensions, the cost of housing or the consequences of a sedentary or indulgent lifestyle. We look at ourselves and at our peers and, on the whole, we like what we see: people who are healthy, vigorous, dynamic and even quite adventurous, and those of us who have retired, for the most part, have no desire to go back into the working world.

> I worked hard for so long, now I have some free time and when . . . I look outside at the rain I think, 'thank god I don't have to go out in that!'
>
> Dorothy Young, 65[2]

We feel free from the social constraints of our parents, enjoying a new sense of liberty that arises out of the magical combination of freedom of choice once we leave the working world and the new scope for individual expression that society now offers us. We may see signs of ageing in ourselves and those around us; we suffer the loss of friends, partners or parents – but we do not see ourselves coming to the end of our lives yet. We still have high hopes of achievement and a full life for many years to come.

The word 'powerless' is sometimes used to describe the over sixties. Although this may well be true of the over eighties, it certainly isn't how we see ourselves. On the contrary, most of us feel very much in control of our lives with both time and resources at our disposal. But just because we see ourselves in a very positive light, it doesn't mean that others see us in the same way.

How others see us

Whereas before we were all but invisible, we now appear to have become newsworthy. The media is filled with demographic reports, comments and analysis of our lifestyles. However, and this is a big 'however', this new-found interest centres essentially around our purchasing power and/or the economic cost to society as a whole of having so many of us around who are no longer 'productive' for so long.

There is great ambiguity in others' perceptions of us. They are not quite sure how to place us; we're obviously not young, but not really old either. They can see we are no longer in the first bloom of youth (or even the last for that matter!), but we are not yet bent over a stick, completely deaf or whatever other negative perception they hold of the elderly. They can't put us into a category because we don't fit into any category that has been officially recognised and named. Indeed, ours is a generation for whom no appropriate designation has yet been found.

This is not a minor point. The term 'teenager' only came into general use when we were children. Before that, young adolescents did not have an identity as such, could not be targeted specifically and their specific needs were not addressed. We, the over fifties and sixties, are today where 13 year olds were in the mid twentieth century.

Unfortunately, the world in general seems to have retained an image of later life, which no longer holds true. Generally speaking there is a telescoping of two quite distinct age groups, the over fifty-fives and the over eighties. All too often 'old' is portrayed as beginning between 60 and 70, and this perception is reinforced by the media and the advertising world, whereas most of us feel that old is 80 and over.

This lack of differentiation is reflected in the literature on later life where late middle age and extreme old age are lumped together under one heading. This is one of the reasons why so many of us find what is written about us as irrelevant and frustrating.

Stereotypical labels such as 'pensioners', 'retirees', 'the elderly', 'old folk', even 'golden-oldie', already pretty negative for the truly aged, are certainly far too generic and evocative of the very old to apply to us. These terms lump together a diverse range of people in an age-span that covers 30 or even 40 years. To be honest, we too have a hard time giving ourselves a name. We may call ourselves the 'new old' the 'youthful ageing' or some other unfamiliar word combination, but we still struggle with definition. Yet in order to achieve any degree of self-esteem and confidence we will have to find a name for ourselves that encompasses the specifics of our age group.

Viewed as 'young-old'

Men still have an easier time as they grow older than women; a man over 60 can behave in a manner frowned upon or condemned in a woman of the same age. Yet all of us are faced with a huge bias towards the young in our society, and also, the cultural messages conveyed by the media tend to conspire against us.

The tone of much that is written and broadcast about us underlines on how 'young' we still are, that is, how we can still run a marathon, play a good game of tennis, have the figure of a 25 year old. By definition this is a negation of the value of age and the contribution age can make. The apparent new emphasis on the older person is still very much based on this underlying paradox. We can be more visible and more acceptable on one condition – that we make the effort to look and act 'young'. Yes, television personalities now admit to having a facelift – but that only goes to prove that looking older is still not acceptable.

Similarly, our society still perceives anyone who is not 'productive' in any way, either as a parent or working, as excess baggage – no longer contributing to society and therefore of little value. A recent morning chat show interviewing well-known people over 60 emphasised how wonderful it was now that we can continue to work beyond 65 and thus continue to be useful. It's a sad indictment of what 'useful' has come to mean. The serenity with which people once accepted advancing years is becoming hard to hold on to.

Viewed as consumers

While we should never forget that two million pensioners are officially classified as 'poor' – which is a disgrace in every sense and an indication of society's attitude towards the elderly – as a group we own more property and investments than any other sector of the population. Since the over fifties hold more than 80 per cent of the nation's personal assets and we are responsible for 45 per cent of all household expenditure, our consumer clout is undeniable.

At first glance it would appear that as a consumer group our needs are being acknowledged. Perceived as having money that we are willing to spend, we are targeted for specific age-related products such as funeral services, stairlifts and health insurance. But, even now, an Age Concern survey showed that 49 per cent of people think the market takes no notice of older consumers. And this is certainly borne out by my own experience. During the course of my interviews, time and time again, I heard the comment, 'I walk into the stores with money in my pocket and there's just nothing for me to buy.'

We do not see mainstream goods, services and products (particularly clothes) which are either made for us or adapted to our needs. There are holiday brochures for retirees, but closer examination reveals these to be the same holidays as for younger people but at off-season prices. The trend towards miniaturisation is the wrong trend for us. We struggle with remote controls that are too small and appliances which are hard to programme. We need things to be bigger not smaller; simpler, not more complex; clearer, not just for the initiated. We are no longer prepared to spend hours peering at control panels, fiddling with impossible dials and knobs, deciding between over-sophisticated options and deciphering tiny print or peering at dimly lit LED (light-emitting diode) screens.

I am convinced that the practice of placing [video recorders] underneath the television makes them visually inaccessible for anyone over the age of 40. To get to the thing to see what you are doing with it requires one to get down on hands and knees, because otherwise you are looking at it through the wrong bit of your bifocals.

Christine, 57

I recently had to return an electric toothbrush to a high street retailer because the on/off mechanism was far too stiff for me. The young person behind the counter demonstrated to me in exasperation how easy it was to use and seemed incredulous when I told him that for someone of my age, the design was hopeless. He made me feel completely incompetent.

Peter, 69

An advertising executive recently made a comment that is revealing of attitudes still prevalent in the consumer world:

A product that gets a reputation for being an old person's brand loses value in the market at large. If I can convince someone of 25 years to drink my coffee I have a customer for 65 years; if I convince someone of 70 to change, I may have a return of only ten years.[3]

Nevertheless, there are small signs of change on the horizon. In Bavaria, Germany, a supermarket opened recently for the over fifties. All shelving is at eye level, there is seating and appropriate trolleys and even magnifying glasses on the shelves to enable customers to read the small (very small) print on the packets. Also, Sanyo has developed a line of remote controls with large symbols, and a number of Japanese manufacturers are developing showers and kitchen appliances for the older person. This trend will surely continue, but there is still a long way to go.

Making choices

By 'choice' we mean the selection from a range of options open to us, in other words making a decision. For the purposes of this book, the words 'choice' and 'decision' are interchangeable. Without getting into a philosophical debate about notions of choice and free will, we can all agree that every day we make choices ranging from the trivial to the momentous. On any given day we may have to decide between cereal or toast for breakfast, or more significantly, whether or not to encourage an elderly relative to go into a care home.

You may prefer to let life take its course and face issues as they arise (in which case this book won't be of much interest to you) but remember making no decisions is in itself a choice, which carries its own consequences. Making decisions is about controlling what happens to us. Not making decisions – in other words, choosing to do nothing – results in circumstances dictating what we do or what happens to us, or others making decisions for us, perhaps in extremis, which we would rather have made ourselves. It is really important that we do not reach an impasse before confronting our ageing years and do the maximum possible to ensure we have some control over what happens to us in every respect.

> My mother was offered a very nice flat in sheltered housing but couldn't bring herself to move in and lost the opportunity. Eighteen months later she had a stroke and had to find new accommodation very quickly and under great pressure. She is now in a much less pleasant environment and we all regret that she didn't make up her mind to move earlier. Of course it

is very hard to act in anticipation of events, but the alternative can be very distressing.

Pam, 52

Often we can't imagine what the outcome might be, or receive so much conflicting advice that we become quite confused, dither and postpone, and think we are making no choice at all. But as Sartre stated 'Not to choose is already to have chosen', and if we do not want to lurch from crisis to crisis or incident to incident, we need to give some thought to the years ahead, making choices with due thought to the future. We don't need to go out and make radical changes, but just factor in the ageing process whenever a decision is called for.

We had to have the kitchen refitted and took the opportunity to raise the height of the dishwasher, get rid of all the cupboards at floor level and just make everything accessible for an 85 year old.

Mary, 64

Mary didn't have her kitchen specifically refitted for her old age, but, given the opportunity, took her advancing years into account.

As we grow older, life reduces the number of reasonable choices open to us (although you wouldn't think so reading some of the literature!) and also our margin of error. We just don't have the number of years ahead of us to recover easily at 75 from a serious financial mistake, to make a new circle of friends as comforting as the old, or to take up an activity that requires years of practice to be satisfying. One aspect of growing older is that many of the choices which used to be straightforward have now become more complex. Choosing from a restaurant menu used to be about eating what we liked best, now we have to think about the medication we are taking, weight problems or the reaction of our digestive systems! So when making choices in later life we need to reflect on our options somewhat more than when we were younger, due to the likely consequences of our choice.

The 'jigsaw approach' to making choices

Making important decisions can be a tedious, time-consuming and unsettling business. We try to be rational and clear-headed only to find that the resulting conclusion just doesn't fit well, and there seem to be so many variables that we can't take them all into account. Most of us, at one time or another, find ourselves having to make complicated choices with all the options going round and round in our head.

One method which has proved its worth and which is used in business management, is the 'jigsaw approach', which involves breaking issues down into manageable bite-sized pieces, examining each one closely, and then fitting them back into the whole. The key to using this method successfully is to give due weight to every aspect of the problem never mind how seemingly trivial or frustrating. 'The devil is in the detail' is never truer than when making complicated decisions. Almost all areas in which we have to make difficult choices fall into one of four categories; social, psychological, physical, financial. Each part of this book concentrates on one of these categories, dealing with issues where one of these aspects predominates.

These areas are like overlapping circles, intersecting and

influencing each other, each one varying in importance according to the issue in question. We often find it easier to verbalise the practical rather than the 'touchy-feely' but often decisive, psychological aspects. So we need to avoid being sidetracked by one aspect and thus failing to examine or give due weight to subsidiary issues.

Let's take the example of Margaret (65) and Steve (68) which illustrates how emotional and financial issues can be inextricably entwined.

Margaret and Steve's Story

Margaret and Steve had a spacious Edwardian house to which they were deeply attached. However, it became obvious that it was too big and they set about looking for somewhere smaller. They found what they wanted but Margaret was reluctant to move and came up with a scheme to purchase the new house while keeping on the old by renting it out. Steve opposed the idea as unnecessarily risky. Margaret's point was that they should take advantage of a very buoyant rental market and make some 'real' money. This situation led to an acrimonious debate and was very upsetting for both of them. I was asked to help and we decided to take the step-by-step approach. Together when we teased out the various strands of their arguments, it became obvious that the issue was not about abandoning the family home; Margaret accepted the necessity of that. Nor was the issue one of financial need, since both she and Steve had very comfortable pensions. A little probing revealed that Margaret didn't want the money for herself but for her children, although both children were high earners. Margaret came to admit that coming from a poor background, she had always regretted that her family had not been able to help her more when times were tough and she felt almost a compulsion to give whatever she could to her children. The emotional, almost irrational factors here were paramount. Luckily Margaret was able to see that her feelings about family, money and inheritance were the real issue, which needed to be addressed separately from the question of selling or renting their home. The house went on the market a week later.

If we had taken Steve and Margaret's dilemma at face value, the issue would never have been resolved satisfactorily; there would have been acrimony and frustration whatever decision was taken. Separating out the interdependent strands of a problem, clears away some of the confusion and provides a structure for the decision-making process.

The step-by-step approach

Here is an easy five-step approach that you may like to use:

Step 1 Ask yourself the questions 'Why is this issue a problem now?' and 'What might the possible outcomes be if I/we postpone a decision?' If you (and anyone else involved) decide you really must make a choice and act now, go on to Step 2.

Step 2 Write things down even if you are not normally a 'lists' person, because keeping things in your head can be confusing. Begin by noting all aspects of the dilemma you are facing in whatever order they come to you, whether they make sense or not, and do this separately from anyone else involved; each person should make their own list. The key to doing this successfully is to be absolutely honest with yourself and include all the possible options open to you even those that are unattractive or impractical. The unthinkable surprisingly often reveals the best option.

You will have now broken the issues down into their constituent parts. So, Margaret might have written, 'house, renting, investment, feeling bad, children, anxious'; and Steve, 'act now, realise house value, obstacle Margaret, frustration, future problems, hassle'.

Step 3 is to sort out the parts into a logical pattern under the headings of 'emotional', 'practical', and 'not sure which', then to discuss divergent points on your lists with the other person if need be.

Step 4 is to examine the issues systematically. From the 'emotional' list, give some thought to what is behind your feeling. Is it directly related to the issue at hand or does it have a deeper cause? Can it be resolved separately and if not, consider just how much weight you want to give to this. In Margaret's case she came to see the house wasn't the issue but rather the need to help out her children. Take however long you need to think through the emotional issues because never mind how much common sense you bring to bear, at the end of the day if these haven't been resolved, they will trip you up and invalidate any choice you make. Do the same with the 'practical' list, considering the financial or social aspects that heavily influence practical issues.

Step 5 is to put the pieces back together by seeing, first, to what extent practical considerations are compatible with the emotional and eliminating the obviously unrealistic or quite unacceptable. Then try to draw some conclusions, and if there is no comfortable answer, make a conscious choice about which of the conflicting elements or aspects should carry most weight. For our generation it is often the 'I should …', 'It's more sensible to …', 'I'll only feel bad if I don't …' arguments that tend to predominate, but there is nothing at all wrong with allowing the emotional issues to carry the day. Write out the acceptable options from best to least bad, realising there will have to be a compromise somewhere. For example, Margaret won't be able to give her children the money she would have liked, but perhaps will accept that they don't really need it. Finally, if at all possible, give yourself some time to mull over your options before making your final choice.

Like Steve and Margaret you may well find that setting out and thinking through all the aspects of a problem in this way, with honesty and insight and giving due weight to every factor, you were mistaking the symptoms for the cause, or that the real issue to be addressed lies elsewhere. This approach doesn't provide you with an easy answer but it does enable you to set out the choices more clearly.

Although in a less formalised context the same approach worked well for Phyllis too.

When my daughter Penny and her family emigrated to Canada, I was really devastated. I had spent a lot of time looking after the children and although I didn't get on that well with my son-in-law, we still did a lot together. When they left everyone said I should get myself a job or take up some activity. They were right of course and I knew I had to get out of the house and meet new people but I couldn't bring myself to commit to anything, I was always dithering and finding excuses why it wasn't quite the right thing or the right time. I was increasingly bored and distressed and in the end had to sit down and think things through. The truth of the matter was that I was hoping to be able to go over to Canada either to join the rest of the family permanently or for extended visits and didn't want to be tied down here. Yet somewhere deep down I knew I wasn't being realistic. I knew the invitation wouldn't be forthcoming. It was really hard for me to face the fact that Penny's life was there and mine is here and that our family ties had changed irrevocably. Until I can deal with that, I'm not going to find anything very satisfying. I'm very sad and I'm still working at it.

Phyllis, 70

'Right' and 'wrong' choices

Unfortunately, there is no foolproof 'method' of making the right choice. We have to accept that we make choices that are 'right' at the time but which may prove subsequently to be 'wrong'. There will always be an element of risk involved. Making any choice needs careful consideration, but of course once you've made a choice, although new opportunities will open, others will close. We can't keep all our options open all of the time.

We talk in terms of 'success' and 'failure' and are heavily influenced by the judgement of our social environment. The yardstick could be money in the bank, material wealth, the number of children or friends we have, or the number of goats or wives for that matter, all depending on our cultural background. But the corollary of this, which can be very destructive and painful, is that we often evaluate past choices with the advantage of hindsight. Take the case of Ellen and Tom.

Ellen and Tom's Story

They decided that instead of selling their car which was still in very good shape, they would make a gift of it to their son and daughter-in-law, who with a young family and living in the country, seemed desperately in need of a second car. A few months later they were extremely upset to learn that the car had been handed on to their daughter-in-law's mother who, they said, needed it more than they did. Ellen and Tom were very angry and bitterly regretted the gift, berating themselves for not having foreseen the possibility that the car might not be used by their son.

In fact, this was just one of those things. A gift is a gift and Ellen and Tom had no way at all of knowing what might happen and could only make a choice based on what they knew and felt was right at that time.

We all have an unfortunate tendency to second guess the decisions that subsequently prove to have been wrong. 'I should have known he would react that way', 'I ought to have read the company report more closely', 'If only I had known then what I know now', and so on. In later life almost all of us are living with the consequences of some decisions that subsequently prove to be wrong, and we continue to punish ourselves for these past mistakes. However, past choices are irrevocable; we made the decision in good faith and nothing can change the choices of the past. All we can do is to try not to repeat past mistakes.

And finally

You may want to read this book from cover to cover or just through those sections which appear to be of immediate interest to you, but since many of the questions discussed such as those dealing with the family or practical living arrangements, overlap from one section to another, you will probably find it helpful to dip as well into other sections which may at first glance not seem quite so relevant. But however you use this book it will make you aware of the choices open to you and more important still, what the likely consequences of any choice might be.

Hopefully, the options and suggestions set out in this book will help you to make informed choices that will still satisfy you over the coming years.

Part 1

Our Bodies

Introduction

TODAY WE ARE HEALTHIER and in better shape than ever before; the proof of this is the fact that the number of centenarians in western industrialised nations is doubling every ten years. Good diet, advanced medical care, our genes and an element of luck combine to ensure that we will live longer and feel better than any previous generation.

Overall, those who worked as managers and professionals will outlive those with backgrounds in manual trades, and women still live longer than men; but longevity has increased beyond all expectations for everyone – and is set to grow further. And just as the number of years we can expect to live has increased, so too has our level of well-being. The onset of symptoms we usually associate with old age, such as arthritis or significant memory loss, now only appear much later in life. Indeed, research has shown that, in any event, such symptoms are not linked to chronological age but to the number of years before death.[1] In other words we only become seriously unwell a few years before we die.

So by the time we reach 50 the odds are that we will probably live at least another 30 years and the question we now face, given this considerable time span, is how much time and effort should we be making to look and feel as good as possible for as long as possible?

From everything I have heard talking to various associations and groups of people over 50, there are definitely two divergent approaches to the way we look and feel. There are those who, in no uncertain terms, say to hell with all the pressures and admonitions about what we should be eating and doing as the years go by, and then there are those who have become very active in maintaining their health and looks. The former can't see any point at all in trying to hold back the ageing process whereas the others are horrified at the idea of 'letting themselves go', as they put it. I personally found myself hesitating between the two, willing to do something to make the best of myself, but not knowing quite what and then having learnt about the 'what', not really able to find the willpower to put it into practice. This is where I suspect most people stand. In the hope that it will help you make some valid choices, the following chapter highlights some of the issues we encounter as we deal with the inevitable ageing process, have increasing contact with the medical world and try to decide if we need to make changes in our lifestyle or whether we can just carry on much as before.

Perhaps a little note of explanation is in order here, since there is one aspect of ageing that is not mentioned in this chapter, nor in this book, which is sex. This is not to say it is either unimportant or non-existent but because, quite simply, it was never mentioned to me except on one occasion and there is little I can usefully add which isn't much better covered by one of the numerous books available on the subject.

Chapter 1

Feeling and looking your best

EVERYONE HAS THEIR OWN ideas on how to live a long and healthy life. Some First World War veterans were interviewed recently by a national newspaper, and I quote:

> Bill Stone is 105 and swears by clean living, a contented mind and trust in the Lord. Henry Allington on the other hand attributes his 109 years to cigarettes, whisky and wild, wild women.[2]

These contradictory replies, which we read so often in the press, are proof enough that there is no magic formula for remaining healthy well into extreme old age, despite what many 'experts' would have us believe. Indeed, research has shown overwhelmingly that it is our genetic inheritance, over which we have little control that has the greatest influence on our health and life span. But that doesn't mean we should leave everything to fate and not give some thought to the question of health, even though we may be lucky enough for it not to be medically necessary.

When talking about our choices in this area, it is important at the outset to make a distinction between health issues (diet and exercise) and appearances (looking good). The two, of course, overlap but the choice of an anti-ageing cream is not on a par with the choice of whether to give up smoking or not. Obviously not all options open to us have the same impact or long-term consequences and the challenge is to be able to evaluate just what the outcomes of our choice may be.

The pressures

It would be wonderful to think that we are really free to do what we want, but whatever our level of fitness, body shape or inclinations, we find ourselves being exhorted to make changes to the way we are. There are strong pressures to do something about the way we treat our bodies, whether on the inside or the outside.

This is part of the trend to make us all more responsible for ourselves, which in itself may be no bad thing, but the implication is that being fit is morally 'good' and that exercising shows strength of character, whereas being overweight and lacking muscle tone is 'bad' indicating self-indulgence and a lack of social responsibility. The pressures come from all sides: the cosmetic industry with promises of a youthful skin after just a few days' treatment with this or that cream, the leisure industry with pictures of the less young gambolling in tropical spas, the family with gifts of health club subscriptions or aerobic DVDs, or on a more serious note, the government and the medical profession tell us what we should – in fact what we must – do. The thrust of this is the message that if you follow a healthy diet you will live longer, and if you exercise regularly you will live more comfortably, which you may or may not believe to be the case.

Some of us already enjoy the challenge of maintaining a healthy body: if you've been a regular tennis or golf player, a keen rambler or a life-long healthy eater, this won't change when you are over 50. And when we retire or the pace of our life slows down some of us will relish the opportunity, finally, to devote some time and energy to taking care of our body. Indeed, you may have already decided that you are doing enough as far as your looks, diet and exercise are concerned.

But for a significant number of us, not to say the majority, the reality is that although we are under great pressure to modify our behaviour, and despite the fact that we are fully aware of health issues, most of us do much the same as we have always done – that is, relatively little, but now we feel guilty about it. We apologise when we take another biscuit: 'I really shouldn't but…' and make excuses to ourselves and everyone else why we don't exercise more or eat more health foods.

Yet most of us realise that as we grow older and become increasingly aware of changes in our body there are some serious choices to be made. If we are not doing much to maximise our fitness it is usually not because we have not thought about it but that we just don't. Now is perhaps the time to reflect on the issues involved and make a conscious, informed decision. Below, under the headings of 'Feeling good' and 'Looking good', I examine the questions most frequently raised in my conversations with the over fifties.

Feeling good – our bodies on the inside

Influenced by the war and the post-war years, our generation was brought up on a plain and wholesome, home-cooked, and often pretty boring diet. We drank a lot of milk, partly because it came free at school, and fizzy drinks were a treat. We had to walk or cycle a fair amount; school sports were compulsory and we spent hours playing physical games in the street or the park. Even today many of us still cook using basic ingredients, make only limited use of ready-made foods and sit down at table to enjoy our meal. We avoid taking the car for short journeys and do a lot of our own housework and gardening, if not all of it. The result is that few of us are obese or couch potatoes.

But it is also true that, unlike the under-fifties, we are not so familiar with gyms, fitness classes or home physical training equipment. We may find the idea of a weekly 'workout' daunting or even a trip to the local swimming pool quite intimidating. Nevertheless, even if we may not be quite so health conscious as the generations that follow us, we do wonder if we are making enough effort to remain in reasonable health. Until recently the choice was pretty straightforward: eat fruit and fibre, swallow some food supplements and we would remain healthy. Exercise every day and we would remain strong and supple. The message was clear: do this and you will be fine, don't do what we tell you and physical misfortune will surely follow. But today we are caught up in a torrent of conflicting views, advice and opinions.

Some recent examples:

- Taking vitamin E has been shown to help the working of the brain, *but* no more than doing the shopping![3]

- Cutting down on salt is a popular mantra *but* new research has shown that this can be harmful and that some of us would benefit by taking more (Swiss research).

- Bread should be eliminated from your diet *but* it can be the key to losing weight. 10 slices of bread a day can help you lose 2 kilos a week![4]

- You must keep your weight down *but* research has shown that people who diet in the hope of improving their health die younger than those who stay fat.[5]

- You have to walk at least 45 minutes a day *but* 6 minutes a day has been shown to be as good as 6 hours[6] and those who slow down live longer than those who exercise.

So even if we are convinced by the 'healthy living' argument, we may end up dismissing much of the information we receive as unreliable or irrelevant to us and using this as a pretext for either doing nothing when perhaps we should be doing something or doing more than we need to.

Smoking and drinking

There seem to be only two issues today on which there is absolute unanimity: excessive drinking and smoking. All health professionals agree on the dangers of smoking and excessive drinking. But many people in our age group, although completely aware of the dangers both to ourselves and others around us, including children and grandchildren, just can't stop.

For more than 20 years now I have been warning some of my patients to stop smoking. I know it is their choice, but not all choices are of equal merit and I tell them so. But to be honest, there is nothing I can say to them that they don't know already. The real question is really, why do some people choose deliberately to harm themselves, and often their children along with them?

Dr Barret, GP

While smoking and excess alcohol are, quite rightly, the subject of huge official as well as personal concern, the habits of a lifetime usually need a life-threatening or life-changing experience to provide a motivation for change. Several people expressed the view to me that they preferred to live for a shorter time rather than remove a pleasure from their lives, and that is a choice of course they can make as long as they are fully aware of, and accept, the consequences to both themselves and those around them.

But if the issues of smoking and excessive drinking are pretty cut and dried, that is not the case with questions of diet and exercise which often remain confusing. Do we need to do anything about either? If we want to improve our fitness, how do we motivate ourselves to start? If we want to lose weight how can we approach this sensibly with potentially long term results?

Thinking about exercise

We all want to be able to walk, move and lift as much as is appropriate to our needs and for as long as possible. Without going anywhere near the concepts of body shaping, extra muscles or flat tummies, let's just begin by looking at the three aspects of exercise emphasised by the Health

Education Authority: strength, suppleness and stamina. Strength to push, lift and pull; suppleness to be able to reach for things and bend over (to cut our toenails, for example); and stamina to be able to do things for as long as we want – this must make sense to us all. And it would seem logical that if in any of these areas we feel we would like to see some improvement, then exercise is the way to get there. So why is it that so many of us choose to do nothing?

Here are the usual excuses we make:

- Exercising is time consuming and we don't have the time in our otherwise very busy lives.

- It needs financial investment even before we know whether we will enjoy it, such as a gym membership, tennis racket or class fee.

- It often means we have to leave the house even when the weather is unpleasant, and we would rather stay at home.

- It is a slow process and we're unsure of the result.

- We can see that people injure themselves.

- We can't see any difference among our friends in either their health or longevity between those who exercise and those who don't.

- We hate feeling hot and sweaty.

- We know that 75 per cent of all people who join a gym drop out after the introductory period, often about six weeks (that's how fitness clubs make their money).

Some of these reasons are valid, whereas others are not, but they all serve as an excuse for a choice that has been made at a different level *not to do anything.*

I believe that the reason for this is twofold. Firstly, the difficulty we have in finding sufficient motivation to get started and make exercise a real habit rather than a daily decision, and secondly, somewhere there is a deep-seated feeling that life will not necessarily be better if we follow the advice we are given. Put another way, that any improvement we may feel in the future is heavily outweighed by the discomfort and effort we have to go through now. It often takes a sudden injury, illness or encroaching infirmity to provide the motivation to do something about our future well-being.

The exercise 'bonus'

There is a point worth bearing in mind, however, which isn't often explained by those who recommend or exercise themselves. We are told that exercising is not only good for muscle tone, a healthy heart and blood circulation, and so on, but also that once we can bring ourselves to make a start, we will feel better – not just physically but less stressed, less anxious and therefore 'happier'. We might assume that it is experiencing the physical effort itself which has this effect, and if we find the whole idea of exercise off-putting we fail to see how the two connect. The fact is that physical effort has a direct and immediate psychological effect by releasing the 'happy hormones', endorphins, into the bloodstream whether you are actually enjoying that jog, swim or climb or not. This effect is independent of what we are thinking as we begin the effort – we may in fact be hating it. But after a short while this hormonal 'rush' has an impact on our mood, an 'upswing' which lasts several hours. It can also be addictive, which is why extreme sportsmen and women have to go further, faster, to achieve the same high that they had before: the more they get, the more they need.

So exercise is not only about boosting our physical health it is also has the bonus of giving us a mental lift, and this is why so many sports enthusiasts are almost missionary-like in their zeal. The upshot is that we may begin to exercise reluctantly but finish feeling better despite ourselves. Getting started is definitely harder than the activity itself.

I had never done any sport in my life, not even really at school where there were no playing fields and we just pottered around in the gym. I had just turned 70 and felt generally out of sorts. So my son bought me an exercise bike and I did that for a while, but it was boring. I don't have access to a fitness centre and the whole idea of mixing with sporty types just filled me with horror. Then one day I got talking to someone who had walked the Pilgrims Way in Wales and although he hadn't done any walking before he set out after just a few weeks' training. That idea really appealed to me, walking with a purpose, with a destination and where thousands had gone before. I began training slowly and now do 15 kilometres (9 miles) at a time. Next summer I'm planning to go off to Wales. I still have a potbelly and I still get puffed climbing stairs but I feel so much better in body and mind.

Norman, 71

We won't all find motivation as strong as Norman's, but if you decide you would like to do more exercise but believe you can't face what's involved, try the following small steps and see how you go on from there.

Some small steps to begin with:

- Stretch all your limbs in bed before you get up.
- Take the stairs at the shopping centre instead of the escalator.
- Get off the bus a stop before your usual one.
- Instead of going to a friend's for coffee, walk round the block with them
- Try small exercises while doing other things: a couple of knee bends while on the phone or pulling in tummy muscles while driving the car or standing in a queue.

If anything hurts, stop. Perhaps you're doing something wrong, or the exercise you've chosen isn't right for you. But don't give up, try something else instead (see below).

A different approach

- Join in some physical activity with others. The social side helps you enjoy the experience.
- Choose an activity which is easily accessible, you need your energy for the activity, not for the journey to get to it.
- Consider joining a yoga or tai chi class. Both these activities are non-competitive and can be enjoyed at any age. Relaxation and meditation are usually included, which provide you with a feeling of well-being.
- Pilates is also worth considering. The gentle exercises are particularly intended to strengthen the spine and to

exercise areas that have been damaged. Again, you are encouraged to work to your own ability.

- Try Aquarobics. This usually takes place in a warm thera-peutic pool. You don't need to be able to swim and the exercises involve moving in the water to music. The classes are often popular with older people and are a fun way to meet others and exercise together in a non-com-petitive environment.

It may be a comfort to know that most of us in our age group get quite a lot of exercise just doing everyday activi-ties such as DIY, shopping, gardening or walking the dog. Unless your doctor has told you precisely why you need to take more exercise and convinced you that this recommen-dation is more than just the fashionable thing to do, there is no imperative why you should exercise more if you really don't want to. And if you decide in the end that you just can't face making more of an effort than you do already, be happy with that decision and make it a proactive choice that you feel good about.

Thinking about diet

I have always enjoyed old-fashioned, traditional food. But I listen to my friends exchanging stories of how they only buy organic food and never fry anything and I feel uncomfortable. They aren't any healthier than I am yet they have this moral halo, which I find irritating. On the other hand, I do sometimes wonder if at some point down the road they will be proved right and me wrong, but just what should I be doing? I am chubby but not overweight and in good health.

Vera, 60

Many of us share Vera's dilemma. If you are overweight and uncomfortable, or are suffering from medical conditions that would be alleviated by changing your eating habits, you have to decide whether you want to go on as you are or whether you would prefer to make some changes. If you are in your fifties or sixties you may be more inclined to make the necessary changes to your diet now, rather than when you are older.

But for those of us who at present are in relatively good health, whose weight, digestion, stamina or strength do not pose a problem, what about 'healthy eating' as in Vera's case? Is prevention better than a cure? Taking precautions against an event which may never happen can be tedious. Knowing, or believing, that medicine can treat most things and that medication for heart disease or blood pressure is today very effective, some of us choose to take the risk of illness rather than take food supplements or make major changes in what we eat. But without making draconian changes, most of us are willing to modify our eating patterns slightly, incorporating healthy eating into our current eating habits.

If this is the case, and you do decide that you'd like to be healthier – and make that your choice – then listed below are some of the more generally accepted habits for healthy eating that persist, despite the conflicting media messages. You will undoubtedly already be familiar with the following, but you may wish to consider adopting them if you do choose to eat more healthily.

- Eat at least five portions of fresh vegetables and fruit each day. Green leafy vegetables are especially important. Fruit and vegetables not only contain vitamins and minerals that keep us healthy but they also contain fibre, which is necessary to avoid constipation – a common problem as people get older.

- Drink water. Try to drink between five and eight glasses a day.

- Include wholemeal bread and whole grains if you can. Brown rice and pasta will provide fibre and will satisfy your hunger – ideal if you are trying to lose weight.

- Try not to eat too much white bread, white pasta, cakes and biscuits, although there is no reason why you shouldn't enjoy them occasionally.

- Try not to fry foods too often. Try stir-frying, which uses only a small amount of oil and is a tasty way to increase vegetables in your diet.

- Try to limit foods that are high in saturated fat, such as butter and full-fat cheese.

The 'feel good' factor

When making choices about diet it is important to give due weight to the 'feel good' factor. Many of the 'healthy' foods we are encouraged to eat are usually low in fat and sugar, which are precisely those foods that trigger our feelings of satisfaction. It makes good sense to reduce our intake of sweet and fatty food but going around all day feeling frustrated and dissatisfied because we no longer put sugar in our tea may just not be worth it. It's important to strike a balance.

Mealtimes are more than just the time of day when we consume food. There are rituals associated with the preparation, sharing and eating of food, which need to be maintained. Now that we are at home much more, these rituals that structure our day become so much more important. So even if we choose to make dietary changes to remain healthy, we should still have a regular time for meals, set the table and take a break from other activities.

Dieting to lose weight

When people of our generation use the word 'diet', they aren't usually talking about eating more healthily, but are talking about losing weight. We can't help but be influenced by the pressure to be slim and that is increasingly true of men as well as women. Almost all of us, at some point, have tried half-heartedly to eliminate this or that food, read about the latest diet craze, admired our friends who have lost several kilos and then commiserated with them a few months later when the kilos go back on! While no one would argue with the need to cut down on deep-fried Mars Bars and ten pints at the local, dieting to lose weight is another matter altogether.

If you are determined to lose weight, whether for medical reasons or not, you need to be very highly motivated to make any meaningful long-term changes to your eating habits, which is the only way to lose weight for good. If you genuinely believe that you will feel better if you shed a few kilos, then dieting to lose a little weight and feel healthier may well boost your confidence.

The problem with most diets that promise a rapid loss in weight is that they restrict food so that the body goes into starvation mode using only a few calories to survive. However, when normal eating resumes, the body is still in starvation mode and so the extra food is stored as fat again. Weight-loss diets also fail to take into account personal likes and dislikes, eating patterns, access to ingredients and cooking facilities, as well as financial, time and social constraints. So it's best to avoid rapid weight-loss diets, but to eat healthily and limit those foods that are more likely to make you gain weight.

All weight-loss diets are much the same: they eliminate this or that type of food or method of cooking, but the simple fact is that the way to lose weight is to eat less. You will choose whether you prefer to eat a little less of everything or eliminate a certain food entirely.

If you choose to diet to lose weight, remember the following:

- You will only set yourself up for failure if you try to follow a diet which is unrealistic or unpleasant. After a few days you just won't be able to keep it up.

- Any radical change to your diet is very hard to maintain, unless there are fattening or unhealthy foods you can eliminate which you don't miss.

- It's much easier to do things with a partner, friend or in a group; join one if possible.

- As with all things, small incremental changes are the most effective, so you should be modest in your expectations. A slow and steady weight loss is more likely to be a lasting one and it will re-educate you into new and healthier eating habits.

Some small steps to begin with

- Begin all meals with a glass of water.
- Eat slowly and enjoy your food

- When you're no longer hungry, stop eating, but remember that it takes 20 minutes for your brain to realise your stomach is full. You don't have to finish what's on your plate – that's a hangover from times gone by.
- Say no to second helpings.
- Change the cooking method not the food. Grill rather than fry, steam rather than bake, use lemon juice rather than dressing or sauce.
- Don't use serving dishes. Set the food on the plate away from the table.
- Get everyone around you to co-operate; ask them not to tempt you with food(s) you don't want.

Health is not only about the absence of illness and infirmity. It is also about being in good spirits and enjoying life. If a change in eating habits makes you moody and dissatisfied, then you won't think it's worth making the change. If a change in your diet to healthy eating, however small, makes you feel and look good, then so much the better.

The straightforward answer for Vera personally, is that if she is happy with the way she looks and feels, then she should resist the pressure to change. The fundamental rule has to be, 'If I feel OK, then I am OK.' Barring a medical imperative, we have as much choice about diet and exercise as about any other aspect of our lives.

So if you do decide that to make a change in diet or to exercise, that's wonderful. If you decide the contrary, that's fine too. The worst scenario is to decide that dieting and/or exercise are not for you but then always to feel unhappy about your choice, making endless small attempts to do one or the other, failing to keep it up and beginning the guilt cycle all over again. Choose what you will do and stick with your choice. Above all, enjoy whatever regime you've chosen. As La Rochefoucauld said 'Preserving health by too severe a rule is a worrisome malady'.[7]

Looking good – our bodies on the outside

As we grow older we want to feel good, and feeling good depends, at least in part, on the way we look. And this goes as much for men as for women. Most people are quicker to respond to the beauty of face than the beauty of spirit, and we are more likely to have someone tell us 'you look wonderful with that suntan' than 'I really admire your positive outlook on life'!

On the one hand we are told that this is the time of life when, at last, we needn't bother with social convention, when we can do what we want and be ourselves. On the other, however, there is constant media pressure to look youthful and be dynamic, right up until we step into the grave. Some of us have greater scope for choice than others.

If you live in a social environment where there are few expectations or pressures regarding looks you really do have the freedom to do as you want. You don't have to follow a dress code, listen to disparaging remarks about people who wear trainers and tracksuits, worry about dressing too young or too old, and so on. But some of us live in a social or cultural environment where there is greater emphasis on physical appearance, where status and social acceptability depend in part on grooming and dressing well. This isn't a problem if we enjoy spending time, energy and money on looking as we are expected to but as we grow older we may feel like Lisa:

> I look relatively young but this comes at some cost to myself. I tint my hair, spend a fair time on my nails and clothes and I wonder if all this is necessary. My friends take great pride in looking great the whole the time but I'm just bored with it all and would rather spend the money on other things. I wonder at what point I can allow myself to show my age.
>
> Lisa, 68

In theory Lisa does have a choice, but in practice maybe not as much as she would like if she wants to continue as a fully paid-up member of her group.

Most of us are somewhere in between – we don't wear tracksuits all week but neither do we spend many hours on grooming every day. We do what it takes to meet with the approval we need, perhaps thinking that we 'should' do more and sometimes wishing we could do a little less.

Coming to terms with ageing

Seventy-five per cent of people are dissatisfied with the way they look at *any* age. As we grow older, we correspond less and less to the image of perfection conveyed by the media. So it's not surprising if beyond 50 we become, if not anxious, at least a little more concerned by the way we look. The ideal is to come to terms with an ageing body and the restrictions that age brings, while making the best of ourselves and the health we still have, but some of us find that much harder to do than others. Unfortunately, if you believe that a beautiful body makes for a happy individual or if you have always relied on your good looks, then it becomes increasingly upsetting to see yourself in the mirror.

We all know someone who cannot face the change, who is distressed by the signs of ageing they see and who spends a great deal of energy denying that they are no longer young: Jean, who wears skirts that are too short, hair that's too long and inappropriate make-up; John, who boasts of beating his grandson at tennis and combs his hair carefully to hide the bald patch. If we cannot accept what we all know in our heart-of-hearts is an inevitable process, we will find ourselves, as Ram Dass puts it:

> Pitting ourselves more and more desperately against the inexorable process revealed in crow's feet, stretch marks and puffiness. We are given two doomed choices, to suck in, thrust out, nip and tuck and build our muscles all to hold onto a semblance of youth or to or resign ourselves in sad defeat, feeling like failures, outsiders, victims or fools.[8]

But coming to terms with looking older is more easily said than done.

> On my sixtieth birthday, my children gave me a surprise party. I was told we were going to the beach but instead they drove me to a smart hotel where all my friends were waiting for me. I know they meant well but I was horribly embarrassed all day. For the first time my friends saw me without any make-up and I'm sure it registered that I was pasty-faced and didn't look my best. Even now I get upset thinking about it.
>
> Jackie, 61

Jackie obviously still sets great store by the way she looks, and since how we see ourselves is deeply engrained by the time we reach later life, she is unlikely to change now. But perhaps you are more like Kay, or would like to be:

> I've often wondered just how much looking good influences what people think of you and I spent a lot of time making the best of myself. But recently I had a sobering experience. I was at my neighbour Ena's birthday party and she looked dreadful as always, her clothes far too tight, her hair in a mess, really not attractive at all. She has a couple of granddaughters at that awkward age, 15 or 16, pretty sullen and hard to handle but when they came into the room and saw their granny, their faces lit up, they rushed over to her gave her a big hug and said 'We love you lots Gran.' They were with her all evening and I thought, well, who you are really is more important than looks and no one cares half as much how you look as you do. It came as a relief really and I have learnt to concentrate more on being good company than doing my nails.
>
> Kay, 75

Making changes

If we feel we would like to improve the way we look, there is plenty of literature out there and it is well worth reading up what the experts say about vitamins and food supplements, cosmetic procedures and generally making the best of ourselves. However, almost all advice is aimed at women even though men too feel they want to look their best. In part this is a generational issue. Men in the under-forties age group spend increasingly large amounts of money on cosmetics, beauty treatments and hair implants, but those over 50 have often been conditioned to think that this isn't a 'manly' thing to do. Today, men who are in their late fifties or older are often reluctant to admit being concerned by beer bellies, wrinkles or lack of muscle tone. Viagra may have helped with men's traditional concern but we are only just beginning to see the mass market open up for a range of men's cosmetics beyond aftershave!

If, as a man, you feel you would like to have a facial, hair treatment or use a skin cream, go ahead, it is now fast becoming the norm. You have nothing to lose and you will certainly have the backing of the women in your life.

Here are some suggestions for both men and women:

- Unless you are especially blessed by nature, looking good over 50 relies increasingly on time and money. Decide how much you have of either, and how much you want to spend of both.

- Do not feel guilty about the resources you spend on looking good. Making yourself feel better by looking better is not a question of vanity but of improving your mental outlook and approach to ageing.

- You can't change the fundamentals of the way you look, but looking well-groomed goes a long way to overcoming the inevitable signs of ageing, the wrinkles, the sagging or the extra weight.

- Pay extra attention to hair, nails and skin. If you are a man shave every day. Facial hair can be a problem as women get older; there are several ways to remove it including waxing and hair-removal creams. Go to the hairdresser regularly. Use the best beauty products you can afford.

- Take a close look at your wardrobe. Is what you wear appropriate for your age? Do your clothes do you justice? Dressing well is not so much a question of money as a question of good judgement. We are not always the best judges of what suits us, and over the years get stuck in a rut as far as style, colour and shape are concerned. Ask advice from sales staff or someone who is not afraid to give you an honest opinion.

- As we grow older our hair and skin change colour and texture so we may need to choose clothes in different shades and styles that are more flattering.

- Ageing looks may well need camouflage. Get professional advice on using the appropriate cosmetics wisely and effectively. If you can't afford a private beauty session, many big stores offer free advice or makeovers.

- If your budget permits, you may want to consider plastic surgery. There are many arguments for and against this and the anti-surgery camp can be quite vehement. But if you are convinced you will look, and therefore feel, better, then now is the time to take appropriate steps. Take your time, get all the advice you can and have the courage of your convictions.

- Learn from others. When you see someone of your age who you think looks wonderful, observe what it is exactly that makes them look so good and see if you can achieve the same. Conversely, when somebody strikes you as looking less than their best or inappropriately dressed, make sure you don't make the same mistakes.

- We all have little vanities to ward off signs of ageing, which is only normal, and it helps if we can view these signs with a sense of humour and keep things in perspective.

- Don't put yourself through the agony of comparing yourself to those who are younger. Looking older is an unstoppable process and you can only make the best of what there is.

- If you are not comfortable with the way your body looks and dislike having it seen in public, you might avoid crowded beaches, pools, Turkish baths and so on, but don't restrict yourself too much. Have a look around you and you will see that most people, even those under 50, come in the weirdest shapes and sizes and you probably conform to the norm. It is far better to be out there with the others, covered up discreetly if necessary, rather than not at all.

We are free to choose the amount of time and money we spend on the way we look but need to do so in the knowledge that sooner or later we will have to come to terms with the fact that we will most certainly look older than we feel. All our lives we have made small adjustments to the way we live to take into account changes in our physiology. As we reach our later years, however, we may find that these changes accelerate, and instead of adjusting unconsciously we have to make conscious choices about what we do. Sometimes we will resent having to make these choices, but if we are to enjoy our later years we need to live with our bodies without seeing them as the enemy – with grace and good humour rather than anger and denial.

Coping with an ageing body

There is nothing we can do about our ageing body. We laugh about it, hide it, are embarrassed by it and just a few of us are proud of it. We each choose to cope with it in our own way, some of us more successfully than others. Some of us prefer to ignore the entire subject. But if you are prone to aches and pains or find your energy levels decreasing or are quite simply becoming more aware of your age, it is comforting to know that your contemporaries are going through much the same process, and many of us share a really good laugh as we recount our experiences.

Almost everyone I spoke to had devised personal ways and means of overcoming the challenge that an ageing body can present and below are some of their suggestions beyond the usual and obvious like getting rid of the lawn, improving lighting on the stairs and so on, which you, too, may find useful:

At home

- On those days when you are tired, in pain or just feel disinclined to do much, spread the work load as far as possible, carry out tasks little by little, stop when you've had enough, pace yourself and conserve energy.

- Do things when you want whatever the time of day. If you can't sleep, get up and use the time. Your daily schedule no longer has to be run on 'office time' and if you want to do the crossword or the ironing, at 3.00 a.m., why not?

- Don't put yourself under pressure; allow plenty of time between activities, visits, chores. You really don't have to finish the paperwork now, wash the car today. Take your time!

- Whenever possible, vary and expand your activities. The more you can change your routine and the more people you come into contact with, the more stimulated you will be mentally and the more physical energy this will generate.

- If you have a choice of new activities, join one that involves some physical activity or where there is a wide spectrum of age. Being with active people who are more physically able than you acts as an incentive to do your best.

- Avoid putting yourself, or your partner, in a situation that makes you 'feel your age'. If you find it discouraging to play ball games with young children, play cards instead.

- Spend less time in front of the mirror and getting upset over more wrinkles and more sagging. You know they are there, so there is no need to examine them, they really don't matter.

- Try the cosmetics that promise eternal youth but don't believe what the packaging tells you. They may work for you, but accepting the way you look is better than trying to alter it.

- If something hurts, give it a rest. Our body has to become a friend not an enemy.

- Avoid eating or drinking anything which you know in advance will bring discomfort.

- Find a painkiller that works for you and use it.

- Wear comfortable shoes. This is especially hard for women because the choice is usually between high heels and frumpy flats, but the key should be comfort.

- Get rid of uncomfortable clothes, or clothes that you are keeping in the hope that one day you will have the occasion to wear them again. They take up wardrobe space and make you feel either guilty or nostalgic.

- If you don't already, start making lists or noting things down. An extra reminder helps you maintain control and your anxiety level will drop. You will be less tense and feel better.

- Don't struggle to carry heavy things home. It takes too long to recover from aching arms and legs. If you can afford to, pay for delivery.

- Rearrange the cupboards so that you are not looking for things at floor level, at the back or in dark corners. You will thus eliminate one of the major causes of a strained back.

- Don't make unnecessary journeys up and down stairs. If need be, invest in a vacuum cleaner, cleaning products and so on, for each floor.

- Don't give in to caution. You have to balance being 'sensible' with getting every possible enjoyment out of life.

Outside the home

- Get yourself a mobile phone and take it with you always; this will give you a sense of security and keep you relaxed.

- Take your own cushion, coffee or whatever essential items will make you feel comfortable away from home.

- Avoid peak travel times, plan your train/bus/underground journeys to ensure you have a seat.

- Budget for more use of taxis.

- Allow yourself *extra* extra time. Having to rush with luggage shortens your life for sure.

- Assume the worst-case scenario: the late train, the traffic jam, your friend isn't there to meet you. Think through the consequences ahead of time.

- Never stand if you can sit – even if it's only for a moment – at the bus stop, in a store. Sit *before* your legs, back or knees ache.

- Conserve every ounce of energy. Put down heavy bags whenever you can, park as near as you can to your destination, even if that means paying for a parking space.

- Learn to say no to events, situations and social gatherings if you are just pleasing someone else rather than yourself and when you know in advance the discomfort will outweigh the pleasure.

- Budget for a more comfortable hotel or B. & B.

If you have discovered a really useful way of conserving energy or making life easier, let others know. It is quite surprising how many of us have found excellent coping mechanisms that remain unshared; we all seem to be reinventing the wheel.

Chapter 2

Medicine and us

···

BY THE TIME YOU REACH middle age you know your body and how it behaves better than any doctor. You know how it reacts to what you eat and drink, and to any drugs that you take regularly. And you know how much you can ask of your eyes, muscles and lungs. You have also probably had considerable experience of the medical profession and know that some doctors are good practitioners and some are not, that some listen carefully and some don't, that some have good diagnostic skills and some haven't.

When we were young the aura surrounding the medical profession was so powerful that it was unthinkable to argue with a doctor and we were expected to obey medical orders without question. But although doctors were sometimes very intimidating, this total faith in their skill instilled a degree of confidence in both practitioner and treatment, which went a long way towards making us feel better. On the whole we were happy to place our health entirely in the doctor's hands.

Changing attitudes

Now times have changed, and so has our relationship with the medical world. Now we are rarely treated by a local doctor from our own community who has known our family for years – an experience which was comforting in itself. Instead we have access to medical care through group practices with complex booking systems and multiple practitioners, where time is at a premium and where we are speedily passed on to 'specialists' or the practice nurse. We are often treated by people whose speech, culture and values may be different from our own, who may not share or understand our concerns and in whom we hesitate to confide. And if we belong to a cultural, sexual or religious minority, we are now quite aware that the same degree of insensitivity, bias and prejudice exists among the medical profession as in the population at large.

> If one is used to operating by the old rules of a warm and caring doctor–patient relationship and hospitals that look after you until you are well, it can be challenging to accept doctors who treat only a small aspect of their patients and hospitals that kick you out as soon as possible for financial reasons.[9]

Health – our responsibility

Today we are told that we must take greater responsibility for our own state of health, a message contrary to the one we were brought up with. We are no longer considered as victims of a poor environment, social conditions or bad luck but are increasingly being held accountable for our own state of health. Smoking, excessive drinking and being over-weight are now seen as socially irresponsible. We will only remain disease-free, we are told, if we follow a good diet, exercise and follow medical and government guidelines. We are only a short step away from being made to feel that *any* illness is our fault, as we can witness in the current discussion as to whether or not to limit health care for those who are obese or heavy smokers. The huge increase in the sale of food supplements and all kinds of over-the-counter medication shows the extent to which we do indeed now feel the increased pressure to look after ourselves and not just depend on our doctors.

In keeping with this new responsibility is that we are now increasingly invited to take part in the medical decision-making process, asked to make choices about very serious issues. These are sometimes medical, involving operations or drugs, or ethical, involving transplants, or life-prolonging procedures. But at the same time a number of factors have contributed to reduce our confidence in medical opinion on which we used to rely so heavily. The increase in the number of malpractice suits with their huge compensation packages, the much-publicised mistakes made by drug companies, our easier access to a plethora of information that can be confusing and contradictory, all make us wonder what and who to believe. Enormous advances in medical science – from embryonic cell research to genetic engineering – also contribute to our feeling that the natural order of things is being disturbed, and that no one is quite in control of what is happening, least of all the medical profession, many of whom appear as perplexed and in the dark as we are.

I have MS and go for regular appointments with a specialist at our local hospital. He always asks me whether I have found any information on the Internet regarding advances in treatment. Sadly there aren't many but he doesn't seem to have the time to do the research himself which I find quite worrying. He's meant to be the specialist, not me.

Jimmy, 58

Questioning our medical care

As far as medical treatment is concerned, our generation in particular has two barriers to overcome. The first is the attitude of doctors towards ageing and the second is our own residual reluctance to question medical practice.

Doctors are still trained to deal with illness and not with ageing; symptoms of the one are all too easily bracketed with, and therefore dismissed as, signs of the other. Or to put it another way: illness is interesting, ageing isn't. We have all heard our doctor say, 'Well what do you expect at your age?' or, 'I'm afraid given your age there isn't much we can do about that'. Age is not an illness, but it is often used as a pretext for not treating perfectly treatable symptoms or, worse still, as an excuse not to spend too much time and effort to find the probable cause of pain or discomfort.

My doctor says the aches and pains I have are just a question of age. I know that's what people say, but there's a cause – so why can't there be a cure?

Carol, 61

Attitudes are evolving and slowly the study of 'ageing' is being integrated into medical training; for example, Dalhousie University now have a compulsory geriatric course for fourth-year medical students, and the Royal

College of Physicians strongly recommends courses on the management of older patients. Nevertheless, research has shown, sadly, that the older we are the less screening, testing and preventative medicine we are offered. We receive fewer procedures and perhaps most important of all, are consistently excluded from clinical trials. Moreover it is still a fact that the tendency is to see patients as a series of discrete body parts each with its own problems and specialist physician. All too often a series of symptoms are not seen globally, in the context of the ageing process, resulting in treatments which are sometimes patchy, incompatible with each other or inappropriate.

The second point is that we ourselves still have difficulty being assertive in the doctor's surgery and even more so in a hospital ward. We may be worried by what the doctor has told us and, from the safety of our homes, express our fears or doubts to friends and family but once inside the consulting room our old attitudes surface. We 'don't want to bother the doctor' so we hesitate to insist that the drugs don't work, that we still have a pain, that we would like to see a specialist or, even more embarrassing still, get a second opinion. It doesn't help that all too often when we ask a question we're answered with impatience and condescension. The fact that we are no longer so familiar with our GPs should empower and embolden us to say what we think. But whereas in theory we try to take responsibility for own health, in practice old habits die hard and we are still too deferential. The younger generations are far more critical, in the best sense of the word, and certainly no longer take what the doctor says as gospel.

When my wife, who had just retired, felt generally unwell and some days could hardly get out of bed, our local doctor,

whom we'd had for years, was convinced she was having difficulties adjusting to a new lifestyle and suffering from stress.
Over a period of about 10 months he gave her all sorts of medication and she must have been back in that surgery half a
dozen times but she still felt rotten. One day our son turned
up, took one look at mum and insisted on taking charge.
Immediately he had blood tests done and they found she had
a serious blood disorder. Sadly she died a year later and I still
don't know if early treatment would have helped. Why didn't
the doctor listen to her more carefully? Why were we so
accepting and passive? I suppose we knew the doctor well and
didn't like to question his diagnosis. It's left us all with a lot of
guilt and a lot of regrets.

John, 73

Our right to choose

Contrary to what many of us believe and despite a health
service that talks about choices but doesn't seem to offer
many, there *are* areas where we can, and should, exercise
some control over what happens to us when we are in the
hands of the medical profession or when we are weighing up
the pros and cons of different forms of treatment. When exercising our 'right to choose', here are some points to ponder:

- Medicine is an inexact science and even doctors have
  their good and their bad days.

- The doctor isn't always right or necessarily even aware of
  the latest advances in diagnosis and treatment.

- Don't keep your worries to yourself. Talk things over with
  a friend; perhaps there is a point you've missed or mis-
  understood. And sharing your worries will give you the

confidence to ask the necessary questions or insist on further investigation.

- If you're worried about the diagnosis or feel a treatment isn't working for you, go on the Internet or visit the library and find all the information you can about your symptoms or the diagnosed condition. Although the Internet can exaggerate problems, you will feel a strong sense of common interest and purpose which is supportive in itself. (The NHS Direct website is a useful one to refer to – see Resources.)

- Act quickly. Some conditions go away of their own accord whatever the treatment, but many don't.

- Pluck up the courage to tell your doctor how you feel. If he or she is impatient, try to ignore this and stick to your guns.

- If you can't face your doctor alone, ask a friend or family member to go along with you. It is very reassuring to have someone who may remember what the doctor has said better than you, or, if you are shy or embarrassed, to speak up for you.

- Ask for a second opinion, or a third. It's amazing how much diagnosis and treatments can diverge. Just think of the consequences if your doctor is mistaken.

- Be proactive! It's your body, your problem and no one will look after your body as well as you do.

- If you are asked to make hard medical or ethical choices, give yourself enough time for reflection, get as much advice from different sources as you can, discuss the options with friends and family and try to separate out the emotional issues from the rational. Although you will take medical expertise into account, you do not have to agree with medical opinion.

Complementary medicine?

I have a group of friends who are all into holistic medicine. I'm not convinced but they are always pressuring me to take herbal remedies, have reflexology and so on. I am quite happy with the medication I take but they scare me with stories of long-term effects. I don't know what to think.

Jan, 57

Jan isn't the only one in a quandary. The debate between the efficacy of complementary and traditional medicine can leave anyone a little confused. However, it is important to appreciate that they are not two competing forms of treatment, but as the name suggests, they complement each other. In many parts of the world the two approaches coexist perfectly well and have done so for centuries whereas in our society, complementary medicine is still all too often subject to debate and we don't always have a sense of the benefit of a combined approach. Many of us have experienced the reticence among our healthcare practitioners in recommending alternative therapies.

Without the help of highly developed drugs we would not be as well as we are today and anyone who claims that the pharmaceutical industry does more harm than good is either misinformed or has a personal axe to grind. Age for age, we are fitter, healthier and receive better medical treatment than ever before. Projections show the same trend into the future so we can be reasonably confident that our later years are likely to be free of chronic disease until we reach a very advanced age.

But we know that the approach of traditional western medicine with its focus on the symptoms of illness and not the person leaves us feeling vulnerable and in need of something more than a box of pills. Many traditional treatments have serious side effects, the long-term consequences of many drugs are as yet unknown and overworked doctors may be over-reliant on drug therapies.

The sense of participation and trust is all too often missing, with doctors making little effort to mobilise our inner resources in the healing or coping process. Modern therapies are delivered through machinery or drugs rather than caring hands.

This is where the holistic approach can come into its own, treating – as its name indicates – the whole person and not just the pathology. While you may have just a ten-minute slot when you visit your (traditional) doctor, an alternative therapist usually spends more time with you, exploring the state of your overall health in detail.

If you are dissatisfied with the traditional treatment you receive, why not consider, for instance, complementing it with something like homeopathy or acupuncture? If you do choose to give the alternatives a try, bear in mind the following:

- You probably have little to lose by exploring alternative treatments. Because whatever practitioners of traditional medicine may say, the fact is that holistic medicine works for many.

- Even if it is 'all in the mind' as many medical researchers state, other research confirms that healing benefits enormously from the patient's belief in the treatment.

- Take the necessary time to find out everything you can about the new form of treatment you will undergo.

- Only take up a holistic treatment with a practitioner who has been recommended to you and whose fees are well within your pocket.

- Never stop your traditional medication without asking your doctor first; the sudden withdrawal of drugs can be very dangerous. Also, some combinations of drugs and vitamins/herbs can be dangerous – so check with your doctor first.

- Find out in advance how long the treatment will last, how often you need to come back and what kind of outcome you can reasonably expect.

- Important! Be aware of the danger that if you become too caught up in the either/or argument and abandon traditional medicine in favour of alternatives, you may be putting off effective treatment until it's too late.

If you, like Jan, are happy with the treatment you have chosen, stick with it and have confidence in your choice. The only question you need ask yourself is this: 'Does it work for me?'

Chapter 3

Dealing with pain

···

I T USED TO BE AXIOMATIC that growing older was synony-
mous with increased pain and discomfort. To some extent
this is true, but far too often we don't deal with our aches
and pains effectively because we (and all too frequently the
doctors, too) are convinced that it is an inevitable part of the
ageing process, which we have to accept. Of course, all kinds
of symptoms appear as we grow older, and we do have more
discomfort but *pain does not have to mean distress* and we do
have a choice in our approach to pain, both psychological
and physical. If we are finding it hard to deal with new or
increased pain, we may need to choose new coping mechanisms and/or new medication.

When we are in pain at any age, it is normal to feel help-
less, that we will never get better, never be our old self again.
We feel discouraged and sometimes even desperate. What's
worse, 'moaning' about it – that is, making it known we're in
pain, is often frowned upon. We are fully aware that in our
society pain is more acceptable to others only if we are seen
to be trying to overcome it. There may be some truth in this

but often it is those around us who would be happier if we did not view ourselves as victims of pain and were seen to be actively fighting against it.

Such stoicism may come naturally to some but certainly not to all, and to some degree this is a question of cultural background. A 'stiff upper lip' was the traditional British way of coping with pain, if 'coping' is the right term, although this applied far more to men than women.

All too often we say as little as possible and cope with pain on our own. However, minimising or not expressing feelings of pain doesn't diminish it, and pain levels are notoriously difficult to gauge since the only guide to our pain threshold is what we say about it. That, in turn, will be conditioned, like everything else, by our past experience, our social environment and our outlook on life.

Deciding when to take painkillers

Aware that we do not recover from ill-health as quickly as we did in the past and that we are likely to have more symptoms in the future, the question we all ask is: 'What can I do now about pain that will bring me relief but won't jeopardise my future health?' Often we are afraid to take quite as much medication as we need because we want to hold it in reserve for the time when the pain or condition gets really bad, so just how do we respond to the question, 'How's your back now?' Only you can judge how much pain you can tolerate but it is foolish to accept any degree of pain that interferes seriously with everyday living, or prevents you from interacting normally with your friends and family. So it makes sense to take what you need in order to feel comfortable. In general, we are very unlikely to become habituated to any treatment, and doctors will certainly advise us if there is any chance of this happening. In any case there are many forms of pain treatment that are not habit forming.

> I couldn't control my migraines. There were days when I was just a body in the room. A specialist recommended a new painkiller drug and I learnt to hit the pills fast and not just to say 'I can handle this'. Taking a drug every day may seem excessive but when I think I used to surrender so much of my life to feeling miserable, months and months if you add it all up, it doesn't seem like a tough choice at all.
>
> Deborah Berry [10]

> I had a choice: whether to take a drug for my condition whose effect is known to wear off after several years' use, or to put up with great discomfort. I decided to live for 'now' and, as my doctor emphasised, a few years down the road there will probably be something new on the market I can try.
>
> Martin, 56

Coping with your own pain

When thinking about pain relief, here are some points to consider:

- Pain can be treated and there is no virtue in being stoic; it is not ennobling to suffer.

- Pain is not a defect; you should never feel guilty about it.

- Putting up with pain without recourse to treatment of whatever nature is a choice. Is this the choice you really want to make? If so, what do you hope to gain from it?

- Pain needs to be dealt with quickly. Yes, it may just go away as it did when you were younger, but it is more likely to become worse.

- Your body is asking for help, so listen to it. It is a great comfort, psychologically, to come to terms with what your body is telling you.

- Organise your life around the pain, don't pretend it isn't there. *Everyone* in our age group has 'off' days.

- Avoid those situations, or actions, that give rise to pain. Never push your luck by undertaking or continuing tasks you know will result in pain. This isn't a weakness. It is a strength to know your own limits. If you know that making the bed is painful, think of alternatives: either get someone else to do it, ask for help in repositioning the bed so you can reach all sides more easily, do it very, very slowly or not at all.

- Don't compete. Physical prowess is for the (very) young. People around you really would prefer to see you at ease in a less-than-perfect garden rather than limping on an immaculate lawn.

- Mental relaxation is the best pain reliever of them all. Try to find some activity – it could be just listening to music or some other 'passive' occupation – that will take your mind away from the pain. There is really no reason why you shouldn't spend the day comfortably watching television if this helps your recovery. For those who have a more spiritual outlook, meditation may also help but will need some practice.

- One of the worst effects of pain is social isolation. If your pain is hard to treat, do still try to maintain as much social contact as possible. It may be hard at first, but unless the pain is truly unbearable, social activity will give you a psychological lift. Knowing that the pain doesn't set you apart from others, the temporary distraction of having to make conversation and the sympathy you may receive helps put pain in perspective and will lessen your awareness of it.

- Understand the effect your pain has on others; talk about it to those close to you and establish how they handle the fact that you're suffering. Explain very clearly what helps you, what is unhelpful and when or why you can't respond as others may wish.

- Know for yourself what you want from others when you talk about your pain: is it sympathy, practical support, helpful suggestions? Or does talking about your pain make you feel better?

Avoid becoming a pain-bore

Talking for more than a couple of minutes, at most, about your pain can be social suicide. As we age we all discuss various aspects of health provision, medication, and so on, more than we used to – but in a general way. When you find yourself going into details of your own personal case, be aware of the negative reactions this may cause.

Jean's Story

Jean is just the kind of person we don't want to become. She is a highly attractive woman in her seventies who can be witty and excellent company. But following a serious car accident her conversation now revolves almost exclusively around her state of health. In the beginning she received every sympathy from her friends but after a time she became a bore and people now think twice before inviting her round. She is fully aware that she isn't as popular as before and puts it down to the fact that she no longer gives wonderful dinner parties. The truth is that there is only just so much interest and patience that people have for others' aches and pains, and like anyone else who only has one topic of conversation, Jean has become tiresome and unpleasant to be with.

Others' pain

People rarely complain to others about the fact that a partner or friend is in pain, but they do have a lot to say about how the person deals with their pain.

> When he's done too much he really feels sorry for himself. He mopes around complaining that everything hurts but he won't stop and he won't do anything about it.
>
> Maxine, 68

> I can see that Margaret has pain in her knees almost every day; she's lost faith in the doctors and I can't blame her. She doesn't talk about it much and although I do my best to comfort her, I feel pretty useless.
>
> Hamish, 70

> When Mel has one of his sciatica attacks, I just keep out of his way. He gets so touchy that life just goes on hold until the pain subsides.
>
> Jennifer, in her 50s

At one extreme, we have the person who talks of nothing else, at the other, the person who 'suffers in silence'. Both can be equally irritating.

Pain is naturally isolating; it makes people tired, irritable, withdrawn, introspective; in other words 'unsociable'. But those who react to pain by clamming up do not always get a sympathetic response from us. We assume – but don't know – that traditional or alternative medicine is not providing enough relief. We see that the pain exists but, as it's not acknowledged, we find it awkward or futile to offer support, and we get frustrated when we aren't allowed to play a role in its alleviation.

At the other extreme, the person who talks endlessly about how they feel, analysing in detail the progress or otherwise of various treatments, can be really annoying, too. We may be aware that people who talk endlessly about their health are often expressing anxieties of a different nature that have more deep-seated causes than the pain itself. Talking over anxieties and unburdening ourselves is definitely therapeutic, but when it is to the exclusion of all else, it is self-defeating. The audience either no longer listens or no longer reacts in a supportive way.

Coping with others' pain

Here are some points to consider when trying to understand how others deal with their pain:

- You can't live other people's pain for them; you can only choose how you react to it.

- If you find it hard to deal with the other person's moods, you can offer help and if it is refused you have to accept that that is how the other person copes.

- It is distressing, but unfortunately necessary, to realise and accept that you can't fix someone else's pain; there isn't always a remedy for everything.

- It is normal to feel inadequate and frustrated about this.

- If you would like to see a change in someone's approach to pain, for example, that they seek different or further treatment or behave differently when the pain gets bad, the time to discuss this is when the pain has subsided, on a 'good' day.

- Explain clearly how you feel and try to work out an approach that works for you both. Don't let irritation turn the situation into a battleground or armed truce.

Emotional support is as important as pain relief, so concentrate on offering sympathy and help.

- Don't try to 'jolly' them out of it if they can't be jollied. It's natural for people in pain to turn in on themselves as they try to cope. Distraction may take their mind off their pain but many people prefer just to withdraw.

- Help them avoid the situations that trigger the pain and be cautious on their behalf.

- Help them to accept inevitable changes in pace and lifestyle.

- If they suffer from lowered self-esteem because they can't do as much as before, emphasise what they can do.

- Realise that what you may perceive as self-pity, an unwillingness to seek or accept help, or a sense of defeatism is probably due not only to the pain but also to an approach to life which is deeply entrenched and unlikely to change.

Joanna and Helen's Story

Joanna told me about her friend Helen who has chosen a very familiar way of dealing with her pain. Helen is now in her mid seventies and always on the go. Everyone knew that Helen had a troublesome back which she usually put down to too much gardening. But recently Joanna and a couple of other friends met up with Helen for lunch and were distressed to see that Helen couldn't stand straight and had trouble easing herself into her seat. When Joanna suggested that she should do something about her back pain, perhaps take a rest for a while every day, this was quickly dismissed as 'unrealistic'. Although Helen's husband is home most of the time, Helen is the one to do all the shopping, cleaning and cooking. She has a large family of grown-up children who drop by constantly for meals and there are frequent celebrations in Helen's home. So another friend asked if perhaps her husband couldn't help out more, or if her grown children could share some of the chores. Helen wouldn't hear of it, and after a fruitless discussion Helen's friends gave up. They felt rebuffed and irritated with Helen and seriously annoyed with her family who weren't doing anything to help.

Later, however, Joanna had a chat with Helen and discovered that in fact Helen had never told her family how bad her back was. She tried to ignore the pain and appear as active as before. Joanna concluded, probably with good reason, that Helen feared she would lose her role as provider, comforter and advisor at the heart of her family and that everything else was subordinate to that, even extreme pain. So it was beside the point to suggest treatment as this would never be accepted unless and until Helen made some conscious decisions herself. Either she would ask for family support and seek treatment for the pain – unlikely at this point – or the unbearable level of pain would eventually decide a course of action for her.

You may be like Helen and choose to minimise any pain you have. And, of course, you must always choose the coping mechanism that suits you and not others. But there has to be a realisation that excluding people from your pain has consequences, and you may, like Helen, end up by alienating those who only want to help.

Helping others to understand your pain

Some explanation of how you prefer to deal with your pain, even if given in a light, off-hand manner, goes a long way to defuse the feelings of helplessness others experience around your pain, and those on the outside must in turn accept their limitations and respect the choices made.

Part 2

Our Minds

Introduction

....

How you approach this section will depend a great deal on how you approach any discussion of things relating to the mind. Many of us who are quite happy to make practical changes to our lives are reluctant to consider making a psychological shift. We may enjoy discussing and reading about psychology, spiritual matters, feelings and emotions, or we may find it uncomfortable, futile or inappropriate. By now our views on this subject will be firmly embedded and difficult to modify. But this section is not only about how to change our mental approach to later years, it also provides a word of comfort, to show that if you are having difficulties coming to terms with changes that you see in yourself or in others, those feelings are shared by many of us. And there are things you can avoid, or recognise, which will make you feel better without necessarily having to resort to hours of introspection or mind-changing techniques.

You have begun reading this book in the first place because you think that you have some choices to make. Also, if you believe that attitude can affect outcome, then you may be willing to modify the way you view things or simply give a little thought to what troubles you, in which case there is something useful here for you.

Chapter 4

A new look at some old values

···

IT MAY BE TRUE THAT as we grow older we no longer care what people think of us quite as much as we did before, but we still need to conform to society's expectations to some degree. In this respect, we are very much influenced by what we hear, read and see around us. At the same time, we may feel under pressure to act in accordance with some of today's values, which quite specifically in later life, are an obstacle to our peace of mind or are unhelpful when having to make lifestyle choices appropriate to our age and circumstances.

Although the proportion of the population over 50 is increasing every year, the values that still dominate our present society are only just beginning to reflect this. Materialism, freedom to act as we please, action, youth and independence, the desire for instant gratification and the pursuit of happiness are just a few current values that are constantly being emphasised, and to which we have increasing trouble relating.

As we refocus our priorities, and perceive that there is a

widening gap between what we are being told we should do and what we want to do, this is the time to re-examine several of the values that are particularly pernicious and see how they sometimes adversely influence our choices.

Independence and self-sufficiency

Two of the most fundamental values of western society (but only western society) are those of independence and self-sufficiency. Although it is accepted that no one is entirely independent, this notion that we should not rely on anyone else in our later years (or be reliant as little as possible) can be positively harmful. We will certainly need help at some stage but often wait too long to ask for it. One of our guiding principles when we make choices about housing, services in the home, how often we should call the children or ask a neighbour for help, is the idea that we 'should' be able to manage our lives on our own and that to expect help from others is a sign of weakness. This value will not serve us well as we grow older.

Choosing when to accept help

Depending on spectacles for reading, medication for good health, the lift to get to our flat or a friend to take us to the shops are forms of dependency that we take in our stride. It is when we need permanent help to do those tasks we did easily before that we feel a loss of pride, sometimes even shame. Inevitably, however, we are no longer able to do what we did quite as easily as in the past. Our choice, then, is to struggle to do everything on our own, to abandon our previous lifestyle completely or prematurely, or to modify our attitude and get someone to help us. Some of us have no problem at all with requesting help, whereas others make a different choice, not in answer to the question 'Can I still do this myself?', but rather 'Shouldn't I, at my age, still be able to manage without help?'

We will most probably postpone getting help for as long as possible, whether from a friend, partner, neighbour or paid service, if only for financial reasons. But it is a shame to see our homes grow shabby because we can't bring ourselves to redecorate, and it is frustrating to have to turn down an invitation because we don't want to drive in the dark. Receiving help can, so often, dramatically improve our quality of life.

> I was tired of seeing Margaret cleaning the house the whole time; it took up too much of her, and our, time. But she wouldn't have anyone in. Then a neighbour came round and said her cleaner was looking for more work and Margaret agreed to take her on 'just to do her a favour'. What a difference it has made.
>
> Mel, 67

Choosing to accept help with grace and thanks is a much better blueprint for later life than an insistence on doing things that are uncomfortable, tiresome or bad for our health. We are not better people for remaining stubbornly self-sufficient when help is needed. One of the most frequent complaints I heard concerning the very old from both professionals and family, was their reluctance to take on the help they obviously needed.

Who should we ask for help

There is, however, a proviso to the above. It is one thing to ask for occasional or regular help from outside – help which can be refused or delegated. It is quite another when we ask for increased help from our partner or from anyone with whom we have a close relationship who may feel an obligation to help through duty or guilt and who, as a result, may grow angry or resentful. Usually help is of mutual benefit but it can also be very one-sided. The growing dependency of one partner on the other, for example, may be lovingly given and accepted without any problem or it can lead to serious tensions, as in the case of Freda and her husband:

Freda's Story

Freda was a lively and outgoing person, but when her husband developed an eye condition that left him partially blind, she found she was increasingly housebound as he became more and more dependent on her. Her friends all encouraged her to go out on her own from time to time and even offered to 'husband-sit' for her; but whenever she said she was leaving the house her husband made a terrible scene and Freda felt she owed it to him to stay. Little by little Freda began to drink until now she is drinking heavily. She admits to her concerned friends that she is alcohol-dependent but says it's her way of dealing with an intolerable situation.

The challenge is to find a happy medium. Although today, statistically it is still family members who help us most, we should never take this help for granted nor believe that it is the 'duty' of those closest to us to help us out. At the same time we must give ourselves permission to ask for help, from whatever quarter, whenever we need it.

Freedom to act as you please

We are often told that a major bonus of later life is the freedom we have to do what we want. At first glance this seems very appealing. No doubt that is why it is so often repeated, particularly by those who are still tied to small children, to a desk or an uncongenial environment. Our society puts great value on individual freedom as reflected in legislation, such as the Human Rights Act, and in the media. But it should be seen in context. Many other cultures, even within Europe, reinforce the collective good rather than that of the individual, and the idea of everyone being 'free' to do as they wish is perceived as running counter to community support and responsibility. Our reality is that although we want to be as free as possible to do as we please, we ask ourselves just how much freedom of choice we really want – and how much we really have.

You may no longer have the constraints of the workplace, or you may have cut down on your work hours. The children are more likely than not to have left home and you may have already downsized, so indeed you probably have more choice now in how you use your time and energy than ever before. But the prospect of endless freedom that was previously so appealing, can now be quite frightening or depressing, especially for those of us who were previously in a structured working environment. Many of us make a series of choices to ensure that we are kept as busy as possible.

Even those of us who have many interests and/or a wide social circle find that we restrict our freedom quite deliberately in order not to find ourselves with too much spare time. But although a significant proportion of us find that time lies heavy and would prefer to be a little less 'free', most of us find we aren't quite masters of our own time and as available as some people would like to think.

Not as free as we appear

There are the constraints of family obligations, the availability or co-operation of our partner and, perhaps most importantly of all, the state of our health and finances. In my own experience, people sometimes think we can fall in with any last minute plans they may have for us and although we may go out of our way to accommodate them, this requires an (unrecognised and unappreciated) effort on our part.

> When I asked a retired friend out for lunch, she hesitated. She said that her days were full of activities and she had to juggle things around to fit me in. She made me feel I was disturbing her routine and I was a little annoyed. But then when we met up I realised she was on library duty, organised a history group, had a life every bit as busy as before and, of course, seeing her just once a year, I wasn't her priority at all. Good for her.
>
> Jennifer, 66

So, it just isn't true that we are 'free' to make up for missed opportunities, take advantage of every wonderful cruise offer, fulfil long-held dreams, but neither do most of us want that degree of freedom so coveted by those who are younger.

The irony is that when we have the energy, we don't have the time and when we have the time we don't have the money and by the time we have them all we don't want to do anything much any more.

Elderly man in a park

In short, at our age 'freedom' is a relative concept and while off-season holidays and spontaneous invitations midweek are a joy, believing that personal freedom is something that will guide us in later life, can be rather vexing and unhelpful.

Happiness

If only we'd stop trying to be happy, we'd have a pretty good time.

Edith Wharton

The pursuit of happiness has become today's mantra and helping others to seek happiness at any age is a growth industry. It is not surprising therefore that many of us believe that now is our last chance to find the happiness that may so far have eluded us. Like the other two values of independence and freedom the idea that everyone has the 'right' to happiness is not universal at all, and to many people in the world the very notion is bizarre. Life isn't about being 'happy', it is about 'living' and happiness is a by-product if you're lucky!

We have been trained to perceive happiness as an ongoing state, conditional on certain events and circumstances, material well-being, and to some extent on other people. Yet research has shown that our degree of happiness is unaffected by climate, money or outside circumstances.[1] Beyond the necessities of everyday life – social contact, food and shelter – the rest has only a marginal impact on our feelings of well-being.

In our society today the word 'happiness' is so loaded with connotations and unrealistic expectations and a permanent state of happiness is such a mirage, that it's not surprising that we feel inadequate and frustrated if, by our mid fifties, we haven't achieved it. We cannot help but be influenced by the advertising and images that surround us, purporting to prove that happiness is ours for the taking if we go on a Caribbean cruise or on-line to find the perfect partner, buy the right mattress or life-insurance. Happiness, we are told, is just a purchase away. We know from our own experience that going on more holidays, buying new living-room furniture or eating out more often give us fleeting moments of pleasure but they do not have much effect on our underlying feeling of 'happiness'.

What is happiness?

We feel we 'should' be happy and we desperately try to make choices that will make us happier. But what determines our level of happiness is so vague, so deeply rooted in our formative years, so dependent on individual personality or circumstances that we would do better to replace it in our mind with the idea of serenity, peace of mind, balance, or contentment. Not a constant warm fuzzy glow, day after day, but the accumulation of many moments of intense pleasure – the fleeting, easily attainable experiences of watching birds at the feeder or hearing our favourite piece of music. Here are some thoughts on the meaning of happiness that may influence some of the choices you make:

- Happiness is an inner state, and to seek happiness through material things is pointless.

- However, this message is contrary to almost everything you hear and see in your social environment.

- Happiness (contentment, or whatever term you use) is a learned behaviour, an attitude to people, things and life in general, not something that you just have the good fortune to have bestowed on you.

- 'Finding' happiness is a misnomer, it can't be 'found' like a lost dog or collector's piece, it is a process. And you will need to invest yourself in this process, if you so choose, as much as if you were learning a new craft or language.

- It *is* a choice. If you decide you would like to be happier, whatever that word means to you, (which isn't quite as straightforward as it seems, since many of us have invested a great deal in being less than happy), then you can examine the many options which are vying for your attention to achieve that state, from the most esoteric of mystical philosophies to traditional religious practice, or simply gardening and taking walks in the park.

> Nobody promised me an unqualified happy ending, but I promised myself a damn good try at a new life and my craziest fantasies have been surpassed. But I won't pretend to be happy when I'm not.
>
> Leonie Frieda[2]

Some of the other values such as youth, action, material acquisition and instant gratification are also hard for us to relate to now, particularly if we are trying to lead simpler, less aspirational lives, and as a result may make us feel marginalised or inadequate. Luckily as our numbers grow and we begin to find our own voice, these values may be slowly modified. In the meantime we will make our choices despite them.

Chapter 5

Who am I now?

· ·

THERE INVARIABLY COMES A TIME when we make a change to our lifestyle, a change that takes us out of the so-called 'mainstream' and obliges us to think about the direction ahead. This might be imposed on us from the outside or at a moment of our choosing, whether it occurs at 55 or 75. Usually, but not always, it occurs on retirement. At this point we find ourselves on different and unfamiliar psychological terrain as our status in society changes, sometimes, literally, overnight.

So many of us identify with the roles we have had since we were young (child, sibling, parent, employee, boss, entrepreneur, and so on) that we have few resources and little idea how to find another.

> When I retired I no longer felt valued as a person. It came as a shock to realise that it was a case of 'out of sight, out of mind'. I had worked with some people for several decades, but I was now a non-person. My self-confidence just plummeted.
>
> Yves, 61

In my interviews I found that, unlike Yves, people rarely admitted this loss of confidence and it was their partner or their behaviour that drew my attention to their difficulty, as illustrated by the examples below:

- Jack (55) accepted early retirement to enable his wife to take up an interesting job some 100 miles from their home town. He spends his entire time working for a multitude of voluntary organisations and has become quite obsessional in his insistence on never missing an activity or a meeting.

- Mark (62) has set out to become the regional bridge champion within four years and spends five days a week at the club or on the road.

- Judy (57) has launched herself into needlework big-time to the exclusion of almost every other activity, going off on every available course and unable to do or talk about anything else.

These are by no means exceptional cases and illustrate a need to find new obligations and structures that replace the feeling of self-worth status so frequently lost when leaving the workplace.

Losing self-esteem

We often read that self-esteem is something we have and then something we lose when we move out of the working world. One day we are part of a team and have self-respect, the next day we leave the team and don't. But it's more complicated than that.

By the time you reach adolescence how you feel about yourself is pretty much determined. If you like yourself and are self-confident, barring extreme circumstances, you will be confident for life. If you do not have that confidence, you may work hard at achieving it but invariably you have put the issue to one side, as the activities of daily life take over and compensate for, or hide, how you feel inside.

So, in your later years, if you are normally confident, then regaining self-respect is a transient problem that you feel, deep down, you can resolve. But if you do not have that self-confidence to begin with, then leaving the working world may herald a distressing period in which you have to address some very fundamental issues: how you see yourself in relation to the world around you, who and what gives you a sense of worth and security, and conversely, what undermines your self-esteem. Finding a new balance may be that much harder to achieve.

Of course, all of us initially will find ourselves in the same situation, faced with the need to feel important again.

But what precisely has changed? Quite simply most of us are no longer in that arena of life that provides the yardstick of acknowledged success: Lindsay's promotion, Chris's decoration for public service, Mina's award for the best sales figures. It is *public* success which excites everyone more than the virtues of kindness or good parenting. Our inner *hidden* achievements go unnoticed.

Our society's idea of success supposes that there is a goal to be achieved, and that there is merit in reaching that goal. But who we are now is not the result of achieving goals. Goals are how we have been taught to structure life but they aren't life itself. We shouldn't be devastated if we don't get to where we thought we should be – we very rarely do. You may be someone who needs an objective, a short-term goal like getting the shopping done this week or a more long-term one like running in the marathon. That is fine if it doesn't lead to a loss of confidence and disappointment if it isn't reached.

Alain de Botton put it very well in a recent article on anxiety:

> We worry whenever we are in danger of failing to conform to the ideal of success laid down by our society that we may be stripped of dignity and respect and from failure will flow humiliation, a corroding awareness that we have been unable to convince the world of our value. [3]

Finding it again

Instead of our status and sense of who we are being determined by *outside* factors, we now have to look *inside* ourselves to find the same degree of self-affirmation, and for most of us that is exceptionally hard.

If our self-esteem has been built entirely on the good opinions of others, we face a real challenge when we are no longer working. It is often suggested that the best way to deal with this loss is to recreate the working world; set up an office at home, take on unpaid work for charitable organisations, keep structured hours and so on. Why not if we want to prolong our working environment in this way as some of us do? But most of us are heartily relieved that we are no longer working and would prefer another form of activity, feeling that going back to where we were isn't a solution, but only a stop-gap.

So in view of the above, what are some of the choices to make you feel important again?

- Realise that if you were a confident person before, you have every chance of regaining a sense of purpose and self-esteem given time.

- If you are someone who never felt very good about yourself, come to terms with the fact that it will take longer to achieve a balance in your life, and try not to feel discouraged along the way – it's not a competition.

- Make a conscious effort to avoid anything that makes you feel less confident. Don't attempt the impossible, don't mix with people (if you have a choice) who make you feel inadequate.

- Make a serious effort to find practical activities that interest and distract you.

- Do what you can to make yourself feel better from the *inside*. Accept that this will take time.

- Take stock of who you still are: a parent, a partner, a friend, a sibling, a good cook, a keen gardener, someone who is decent, reliable and capable. These are all of great value, and you should regard them as such.

- Put aside notions of happiness, success, or failure. They're unhelpful and no longer relevant.

- By all means set yourself goals, but make absolutely sure these are realistic because achieving a small goal is infinitely better than failing to reach a greater one.

- Understand that doing nothing is *not* a waste of time, but being unhappy about doing nothing *is*. Because when we do 'nothing' we are doing something: looking out of the window, staying warm in bed, watching television. As long as you feel good right now, ignore all other pressures.

- Once you leave aside the idea of goals and the virtue of achieving something tangible, you will realise that no one activity is better than any another.

- However, if you're doing nothing when you would like to be doing something but can't find the enthusiasm or energy to begin, then you need to ask yourself what it would take for you to change things or to feel better – and answer realistically!

- It could be that you need the encouragement of a family member or someone close to you. Ask for their help.

- It could be that a small change in your mood will enable you to find the necessary impetus to take the small step to put you on the right road. Maybe this mood change can be induced by a non-habit forming substance which would give you just the necessary lift to spur yourself on, for example, a herbal mood enhancer such as St. John's Wort.

- Or – yes, this is possible and allowed – see your doctor and discuss whether a course of mild antidepressants may help you in the short term. Or see a counsellor. Building self-esteem isn't something we can always do for ourselves and there is no shame attached to asking for help. Many people do.

I often see retirement-related problems and wish people, especially men, would seek help sooner. When people stop work they make a radical change in lifestyle and it's only normal that there will be a period of adjustment both mental and physical. Any opportunity in whatever form, to share their thoughts is invaluable; it's not work that has to be replaced but the sense of belonging.

Sandra P, psychotherapist

- Remember all the times when you felt good and were made to feel you were of worth.

- Reinforce relationships with people who make you feel good and let go those relationships that don't.

- Explore spiritual avenues, new philosophies of life that do not depend on outside sources of reinforcement and esteem (see Chapter 8 on Spiritual life).

- If you feel you can't do without some form of outside recognition, take on some organisational responsibility for a group or charity. Volunteer your services where you can put old skills to good use, or develop new ones. A first step may be to go on the Web and see all the organisations that are looking for help (see Resources).

- Don't belittle any of the activities that bring you a sense of satisfaction. Do whatever makes you feel good – however small, 'ridiculous' or 'futile'.

- Don't denigrate yourself when people praise what you are doing or have done.

Chapter 6

Regrets of the past and fear of the future

SOME ROADS CAN NEVER BE rediscovered. You lose your virginity once. You have one fleeting season to be sixteen in Paris in the spring. Decisions have a way of being made and life lived in peculiar ways and some dreams are lovely only because they can never be realised. They live where they belong – in our glorious fantasies.[4]

Regrets of the past

For many of us, life has been a series of compromises, obstacles, disappointments and re-evaluations. The flip side to these are the good times, lucky breaks and moments of pleasure. From the day we are born we are more favoured or less favoured by life, and if some of us feel we've had more than our fair share of bad luck and hard times or didn't get the recognition we deserved, objectively this may well be so. As we all know, life is not about fairness.

We have all failed at something. It is how we feel about

that failure that differentiates us. The past is irrevocable but perhaps we are still living with the consequences of our 'failure' – or lack of success. We wish we had made more money, had children, taken better care of our health. This can cast a blight on our lives.

You have no choice over past failures, they cannot be changed or relived. Life has moved you on and most of your failures you probably perceive only with hindsight. You might well have done better if you had continued with your studies, or been happier if you had married Mary instead of Sue, and so on, but this second guessing is futile. You have to stop judging the person you were in the past. But although we know that it is unproductive to review the past if it only brings self-reproach to the fore rather than happy memories, it isn't at all easy to change your psychological approach. It takes some mental acrobatics to gain a balanced perspective. The choice that faces you now is either to continue to dwell on your failures and allow them to undermine your present state of mind, or to say, 'Yes, I would have done better if', or 'Yes, I should have given it my best shot', and then put those unfortunate choices definitively to one side. It *is* possible to free yourself from regrets if you so choose and as always, the real issue isn't about *what* to do but *whether* to do anything. An easy first step to take is to read one of the books suggested in the Resources section.

At a time when we are facing myriad choices that will have long-lasting repercussions for the future, grief over unfulfilled hopes and wishes, and energy misdirected towards what might have been, can only lead to dissatisfaction and an unsatisfactory lifestyle. We can't forget our failures but should allow them only a small walk-on part in the drama of our lives.

When people talked about the 'rich tapestry of life' I had always found that expression pretty trite. But my grandson had a bad experience at school the other day and, as it happened, I was doing a piece of sewing when he told me about it. I showed him that on the 'right' side of the work everything looked neat and tidy but when I turned it over he could see the knots, the loose ends and the tangles, yet one side was part of the other, there was no way of separating the good side from the bad. He accepted the idea at once and I hope that image will help him in the future.

Beverley, 60

Fear of the future

It is perfectly normal as we grow older that we should be anxious about what lies ahead. Old age hasn't had a good press and although we aren't there yet, we see it on the horizon. Our fear may be based on our perception of ageing and old age, which we envisage as being unpleasant, a source of pain or discomfort. If Alzheimer's or a certain form of cancer runs in the family, some of our anxieties may be fully justified, and if we have seen distress around us among the very old, it is normal that we feel anxious that this shouldn't happen to us.

We are not talking here about clinical depression or obsessional anxieties that take over our lives completely. These are conditions which need professional help. Rather it is about the floating state of anxiety about everything in general and nothing in particular, which many people I questioned admitted to. It is perfectly normal that when we make the transition from one stage of our life to the next we should feel vulnerable and confused and full of fears, many of which we know are irrational but which we can't rid ourselves of. Here are some examples:

- I used to run to catch the train, I now make a point of getting to the train with an hour to spare.

- Mark has taken to checking all the car doors twice over now even though we have central locking.

- I never used to worry about my health but now when we travel I am more concerned about health issues than the destination.

We are told to 'trust in the future' and in our ability to manage the unforeseeable. But this sense of trust i.e. the feeling or conviction that things will unfold within a dependable and manageable framework, is not something that comes easily to those whom the past has not treated kindly. It is not solely a question of conscious choice. The capacity and will to trust is influenced by our individual life experience, and not all of us are able to view the future positively.

Dealing with worry

You may have spent all your life as a worrier, full of anxieties about what 'might' happen. In later life this is unlikely to change much, unless you want to put in more effort (or therapy) than most of us are prepared to do at this point. It is only when these anxieties become overwhelming and prevent us functioning normally that we need to address them more seriously.

If you want to deal more effectively with your fears you

will have to change your patterns of seeing, thinking and behaving. This will require considerable commitment but may be worth the effort. There is a mass of literature on fear and anxiety, which helps put fears in perspective and offers practical suggestions for changing how you think, such as Dr Susan Jeffers's suggestion in her best-selling book *End the Struggle and Dance with Life*. [5]

> Set as many goals as you want. Picture exactly what you like to happen. With loving effort do the work necessary to bring the desired results to fruition. And when you are satisfied that you have done as much as you can, LET GO OF THE OUTCOME!

As well as reading what she and other 'experts' say, you could try some of the strategies listed below which other chronic worriers told me worked well for them:

- Be conscious of the fear, bring it to the fore rather than allowing it to stay nagging at the back of your mind. Pretending it isn't there doesn't work.

- Examine your fear(s) close up; make a list if necessary. Which are the real, practical worries, and which are formless anxieties? Can you look for any practical solutions to concrete problems? If you can, do so. This will lessen the overall burden.

- If anxiety is limiting your life, talk to a counsellor. Or ask your doctor for help through medication.

- If your fears become obsessive, seek professional help. Katy (now 62) told me how in her mid fifties she developed an irrational fear of bears or any image of them, which ruined several family Christmases. But after just a few sessions of appropriate therapy, she could walk happily into a toyshop again.

- Explore new ways of calming yourself: yoga and mediation can be learnt at any age; a back rub can literally lift the load off your shoulders. T'ai chi exercises are recommended by many.

- Talk to a sympathetic friend; sometimes just voicing fears reduces their impact.

- Share your fears with others to see how they cope with theirs.

Remember

Fear of the future is fear of what might happen to us and to those dear to us that is beyond our control. It is about imagined events and not about reality.

While it is true that we can learn, by making intelligent choices, not to make things worse for ourselves in certain ways, there are many things in life over which we have little or no control. We do not have to be victims in the face of large forces in our lives. We can learn to work with them, understand them, find meaning in them, make critical choices and use their energies to grow. [6]

Chapter 7

Changing relationships

··

THE IMAGE OF DARBY AND JOAN, sitting side by side, happy in each other's company in their twilight years, has its place – but only on top of a chocolate box. We would love to remain together hand-in-hand with our partner until we both simultaneously disappear. But sadly, the chances that we grow old in sympathy and in sync with our partner and contemporaries are small. While most of the time we are perfectly happy to offer support and comfort to partners and friends as time passes, there are invariably occasions when we become frustrated and irritated, and downright worried, when we become conscious of an 'ageing gap'.

Our ageing partner and friends

Within any relationship one person may look or behave considerably older or younger than the other and we accept this as quite normal until this is coupled with physical changes, and we become aware of inappropriate behaviour or signs of physical ageing that distress us.

> I was always very proud of the way Harry looked but he is getting really overweight now and doesn't seem to care. I find it almost embarrassing to go out with him because he just doesn't do himself justice.
>
> Binnie, 62

> I wish my friends were a little more adventurous but they always find a reason not to try something new; we go to the same restaurant time and time again and although I love them dearly, I'm beginning to find them boring.
>
> Denis, 59

It isn't the onset of serious and chronic illness that upsets us. Indeed, when we see those around us struggling with serious health problems we are full of sympathy and offer our support willingly. Rather, it is the small incremental changes that we can find distressing. We are painfully aware, for example, that she wears too much make up for her age, or that he is getting a real beer belly. What was an amusing little characteristic when someone was young and still just about acceptable when they were in middle age, is now an intolerable strain on the relationship. Our tolerance level seems to drop and we find it harder to accept others' 'bad' habits, although we know that things are unlikely to improve.

If we have a live-in partner, we see our own ageing mirrored in them every day, both physically and mentally. This can add to the strain that many of us experience within a relationship when we are thrown together for the best part of the day. So much so that some of us are tempted to leave our partners at this point, either in the hope of finding someone else more stimulating, or just to be free to lead the life that our partners won't or can't lead with us.

The statistics are eloquent. While the overall divorce rate in the UK has dropped 8 per cent over the last ten years, divorce among the over sixties has risen by 20 per cent. The majority of these divorces are initiated by women, which disproves the theory that it is men who leave their partners in search of someone younger. The reasons given for this rise are various: the greater financial independence of women, the realisation that we may have 15 or 25 years of active life ahead of us after retirement, our greater expectations of life, the social acceptance of divorcees and the idea of an active sexual life in later life. These all contribute, not so much to marriage breakdown, but to the growing alienation within couples whose partnership was already unsatisfactory when they were younger. Fewer people today accept boredom and routine for old times' sake.

Ray and Patty's Story

Ray and Patty had a fairly stable marriage but now in their early sixties they are beginning to find life together rather tough. Patty was always very emotional but now she sees drama at every turn and Ray is growing increasingly exasperated with the endless tears and emotional outpourings. Craving a quiet life, he has started going off to do odd jobs for anyone who asks, just to get away from the house. This infuriates Patty who feels she is not getting enough support. Ray is now talking about leaving to go and live with one of their daughters.

Ray has a very hard but very significant choice to make. He can certainly walk away from what he thinks is an impossible situation; many thousands of people do just that. But late divorce or separation is primarily a solution to abuse, irresponsibility, drug or alcohol problems or when the partnership has been unsatisfactory for many years. Ray and Patty's circumstances are fairly common; many of us find ourselves living in uneasy domestic circumstances but we nevertheless remain with our partners.

We have to accept that our partner is ageing just as we are, and that we need to help each other in adjusting to the process, making ourselves more comfortable with the faults and weaknesses on both sides even as they become more evident.

If the physical and mental changes we see in our partner or friends are beginning, or continue to worry us, the choices open to us are based on the fundamental principle that later in life people really don't/can't/won't change. We don't change a great deal when we are younger either, but it takes us some time to realise that!

How we deal with ageing in others

Given that we can't expect much change, we can only choose to alter the way we ourselves see and deal with the situation, and try to make small modifications that will ease some of our irritation or frustration.

The following are some suggestions and choices to make ourselves more comfortable with ageing in others:

- Accept that very few people age in the same way at the same time; accepting that our friends and/or partner is ageing is not a form of defeat, this isn't a battle about who can stay youngest the longest.

- You see signs of ageing in others and maybe those wrinkles or lapses of memory distress you, but perhaps your friend or partner *isn't* growing older more quickly than you, it's just that you can see *their* face/*their* bad habits, but not your own.

- Realise that if you find others irritating or upsetting, the chances are the feeling is mutual.

- If you know someone is having problems with ageing, be discreet about suggesting help to do the jobs they used to take in their stride; do what you can to bolster their ego.

- There is no point drawing attention to any signs of ageing that can't be changed. If the problem has a remediable cause, however, such as failing eyesight or hearing, do whatever you can to get the problem corrected. (More people complained to me about deafness in others than about any other symptom.)

- It may be possible to talk things over. It is hard to give up an irritating habit but it may be possible to reach a compromise. You both have annoying habits, so why not agree that each of you will make an effort to give up one 'bad' habit? You will turn the landing light off in exchange for your partner putting the lavatory seat down.

- If the problem can't be resolved through discussion for whatever reason then you need to change how you react to the situation.

- If you face a daily irritation see if the situation can be circumvented.

> He always makes such a mess of eating spaghetti. I hated watching him spill sauce all over the place, so I have given up serving it.
>
> Hilda, 58

> She is a terrible backseat driver so I either let her drive or go out on my own.
>
> Terry, 70

- You can try to cajole someone into doing what you want but this can be tiring and lead to resentment. You may wish to look for someone else to accompany you, or get used to doing certain activities alone.

- A fine balance has to be found between making allowances for others' reluctance to do something and encouraging them to make the best use of what resources they do have.

- Avoid those situations that highlight your divergent expectations. Going on a hiking holiday, or a shopping spree when they tire more easily than you, makes no sense.

- If your partner or friend doesn't want to do something, it doesn't mean you can't do it. You don't have to act as 'old' as or 'young' as someone else.

- Give yourself permission to do something on your own. If you feel guilty, or are made to feel guilty about this, examine why this is and realise that you do have options.

The choice of acting independently can be a very hard one and not everyone wants to make it *but it is an option.*

- Similarly, ask yourself what stands in the way of your partner acting on his or her own. Are you making it difficult for them to leave the house, drive the car? Do you feel you are failing in some way if you do things separately?

- Compromise; a little is better than nothing.

Much older or younger partners

My sister married a man much older than herself. He is now 85 and she is 68 and they are both having a hard time. Lisa realises that she will soon be widowed and is insistent that they sell their house and move into something she can manage on her own. Jim wants to die in his old family home. Lisa wants to go out and enjoy herself but Jim just doesn't have the energy any more. In a way I see Lisa anticipating widowhood while Jim is still alive, and he knows that.

Robbie, 66

I feel sorry for Betsy. She is 15 years older than her husband and until recently this wasn't an issue. But now that she is 65 and he is 50, she seems under pressure to stay young. She dresses too young for her age, really can't keep up with his sports activities and I know she's worried about the next ten years. He still has a roving eye and I don't know what I would do in her shoes.

Greta, in her forties

Sometimes a big difference in age, which wasn't really noticeable in our forties and fifties, becomes more obvious and more worrying in our sixties or seventies. When there is a considerable age gap between partners, they have to deal with issues beyond those facing most couples as they age. None of these are particularly easy to resolve, especially if the issues aren't addressed openly.

Synchronised emotional and physical stages are the backbone of any relationship, but when there is a significant age gap there will inevitably be moments when there is a noticeable divergence in needs and preferences. There are issues of health and energy levels and the psychological approach to future years. The perspective of someone in their seventies is not the same as that of someone in their fifties.

One partner may feel that they want to wind down, while the other resents what is perceived as a withdrawal from active life. There may be divergence over spending patterns when one partner is still anxious to acquire while the other is content with what there is, or even anxious to start handing things on to the next generation. Socialising may be stressful when one partner tires easily or socialises less. There are issues of the home. If it is adapted to the older person it makes the younger feel that they are living in an inappropriate environment, or if there is a change of housing it may suit one far more than the other. The younger partner may want some provision to be made for what they see as an inevitable period of bereavement and subsequent solitude, and try to pre-empt future loss by establishing a lifestyle which doesn't include the older partner. This 'role rehearsal' is one way of coping, but one of the difficulties in anticipating life alone in this way is that it may come too soon for the older partner who feels excluded and already buried.

Talking about what will happen when the older partner dies may seem insensitive and morbid, but the alternative, pretending it won't happen, can be quite frightening and leave the younger person feeling very vulnerable. In my conversations a significant number of women who are considerably younger than their partners were already thinking in terms of being on their own, although their partners still had many years ahead of them.

Men who had older wives tended not to refer to this problem. One interviewee said that, as a couple, he and his much older wife had met with so much disapproval in the beginning that now they were very careful never to reveal their ages. Proof, if needed, that marrying a woman older than you is still not as acceptable as the other way around.

The greatest difficulty comes when the younger partner finds they must take on the role of carer while they are still relatively young and want to be free and active.

> I always said that you marry 'for better or worse', and I really believed that. I am now faced with the worst, and silly phrases don't do much good. The reality is that I resent giving up my time and spending all my energy being nursemaid. Everyone talks to me in terms of duty and paying for the good years and all that stuff. Well, I've had enough. I'd like some sympathy once in a while.
>
> Teri, in her mid fifties

Looking at the choices

One of the pillars of a happy, stable relationship is the idea that one partner can count on the other for support through difficult times, that there will be a sharing of the bad as well as the good. But the knowledge that the younger partner almost inevitably will be facing the future alone and may have to act as carer for quite some time, can make for some very stressful last years together.

When difficulties associated with the age gap are addressed openly, the situation is far easier than when there is a pretence that age makes no difference. Resolving some of these issues will need strong communication skills, dedication, honesty and a lot of effort, but they need to be discussed and answers found – before the fact and not after.

If you are much younger:

- Talk about how you feel.

- Realise that even in couples of the same age, one partner usually has to take care of the other at some point.

- Encourage your partner to help you with plans for the future.

- If your partner won't address your concerns, make your own plans. There is no need to feel guilty or disloyal about this. You have to establish some control over what will happen to you.

- Once you've made some decisions, don't talk about your future endlessly in front of your partner.

- It is normal to go over in your mind all the scenarios that may happen around your partner's death. You may begin the grieving process early, while they are still alive, which is not uncommon.

- However, try not to impoverish your last years together by withdrawing too soon emotionally. It is natural to want to protect yourself, but this shouldn't be at a cost to your existing relationship.

- You need, and should develop, your own sources of satisfaction.

- If the situation is distressing you and you are finding it hard to deal with your conflicting emotions, seek outside help. Your position is intrinsically stressful, so don't blame yourself or feel guilty for feeling frustrated or anxious.

- Don't be influenced by what anyone says you should or should not do. Only two people count, you and your partner, and both your needs have to be addressed, although one may take priority over the other.

My friend's husband was a good 20 years older than she was. She absolutely insisted that they move back to her home town where he was truly miserable. He died just a couple of years later at 85 and my friend said that proved she had been right all along to insist on the move. I'm not suggesting there was an easy solution, but in my mind there is no doubt that he sacrificed his last years for her and then chose to bow out.

Gerry, 59

If you are much older:

- Encourage your partner to be more independent if that is what they wish or need.

- Allow there to be discussion of what will happen when you are no longer around.

- Act on what you both decide; this may be harder for you but it is your partner who will have to live with the consequences of your joint choices.

- Let go of any guilt you may have about no longer being able to keep up with the other's energy levels. Everyone growing older has symptoms of ageing.

- Don't try to act your partner's age, it is frustrating and demeaning.

- When your lifestyles become incompatible, allow each other as much space as possible.

- Reserve any energy you have for time you spend together.

- Take on as much help as you can afford. You will feel less guilty about not doing things yourself anymore and your partner will not be carrying an extra burden.

- Give yourself permission not to take part if there is an activity involving lots of younger people or requiring a lot of energy.

- Give your younger partner their freedom. Turn a blind eye sometimes to what may be happening outside the home. It is neither fair nor realistic to expect them to give up something important because it can no longer be done with you.

- Don't oblige them to share an 'older' lifestyle.

- Express your own needs, desires and fears. It's easier to compromise and be generous towards the other person when you know you are also getting your fair share of support and consideration.

- Make as many allowances as are necessary to overcome the ageing gap. Agree to any changes to sleeping or living arrangements your partner may request without a fuss.

I've enjoyed my wife being younger for many years, she's made things brighter and happier for me for a long time, there's no doubt about that. I don't see so much of her any more now that I'm housebound and she gets on with her own life, but that's a fair price to pay for the time she's spent with me. There's a cost for everything.

Henk, 86

A final thought

'Respect your age whatever that chronological number happens to be. Secondly, understand and respect the reality you find yourself in, including whatever circumstances you haven't the power to change. Third, recognise what's within your power to change and learn effective ways to accomplish this. And finally remember that what is always within your power is the ability to modify your attitude towards a person, circumstance or an event.' [7]

If your partner is ill

I am confined to the house quite a lot because my partner is very ill and we spent Christmas alone. I felt terrible as I saw everyone around me seeming to have a really good time. The worst was when people asked afterwards what my Christmas had been like. I didn't have the courage to pretend and told them straight out it was pretty dreadful, that I'd watched the telly and only got one telephone call from a friend abroad to wish us happy Christmas. I was rather surprised by the response I got. Some people I spoke to said they had been on their own too, feeling out of things. Perhaps next year I'll think about contacting some of them.

Lysette, 77

The difficulty for Lysette lies in the fact that she is not living on her own and can't do whatever she wants. People who need to be cared for or who are less sociable than we are, can cut us off from others.

If you feel you are having to choose between your duty to someone else or to yourself, consider this:

- Never mind how much the other person needs you; you also have a duty to yourself. If you are lonely and unhappy you will not be able to take good care of someone else.

- It follows, therefore, that time for yourself is not a luxury but a necessity.

- It is essential to find an activity that satisfies you.

- It will also require some courage on your part to say that you will be away for a while, or pursuing an activity that does not include him or her.

- This may not happen overnight and you will only succeed if you are determined to change your social environment.

- If you meet great resistance, enlist the help of the doctor, a friend or relative to help you put forward your point of view.

- If you really can't leave someone alone, maybe there is a person, service or organisation that can help. There is frequently more help out there than we first realise.

Take a first step, anything at all, however small, to break your isolation.

Chapter 8

Loss and feeling lonely

THE TWO GREAT FEARS OF later life are to lose what we hold dear and to find ourselves alone. Many of us prefer not to dwell too much on these fears in the hope that they may never happen, but they give rise to too much anxiety for the subject to be ignored. Even if we feel able to cope with these situations, many others around us can't, and we need to think how best we can give and find help.

Loss

We know that loss is an integral part of life, and that as we grow older our losses will increase in number and frequency. We will lose many things big and small: friends and family members, earning potential, perfect health, our looks, and so on.

Bereavement is the most obvious form of loss at any age and for which we will probably get most help; our social network, organisations and the enormous amount of literature on the subject are sources of support and sympathy. Strangely enough, however, when talking to the many people who shared their experience of loss with me, bereavement was mentioned only in passing. It was there in the background but perhaps because it happens to us all and the pattern of mourning is so widely discussed now, there wasn't much anyone felt they could add to the debate. The practical and psychological support people had received was, on the whole, adequate if not always appropriate.

Other losses

What did emerge from these discussions, however, was a degree of distress, a feeling of guilt and frustration, about a loss which it isn't 'done' to dwell on, let alone solicit help for: the loss of a pet, physical attraction, chats in the staff canteen, reading without glasses, money lost through poor investments – these were all mentioned to me as losses that were felt very keenly. Loss is inevitable but it is acceptable to talk quite openly about some forms of loss, yet not about others.

Little help is on hand when a pet dies, when we can no longer keep up with our hiking group, lose our own teeth, when we realise that we will not marry (again) or be able to have children, losses which we may feel as much – dare I say it – as the loss of a person.

When my husband died I received a great deal of support. I was quite surprised really just how kind people were. Of course it took time to grieve but I came through it and now on the whole manage quite well. But when my beloved cat died it was quite a different story. I couldn't tell anyone just how attached I was to her, nor how much I missed her, and I felt foolish and almost ashamed that her loss was almost the same as losing my husband. It's OK to love your pet, but it's not OK to show that much grief when it dies.

Lindsay, 66

When a child dies, help and sympathy are immediate. When a child emigrates to the other side of the world, the reaction is 'Isn't that exciting for her!', 'How wonderful for you, you can have some wonderful holidays there.' When a new building blocks your favourite view, where do you find comfort? When friends, for whatever reason, can no longer visit you, or you visit them, what compensation is there for the loss of their company?

These losses are tangible, there is a physical absence. But there is also the psychological loss of dreams and hopes, the realisation that we will never make it to the moon or on to the catwalk. That the many things we had hoped to do will never be done.

Even though (our) dreams may be silly to others, they may have given us psychological warmth and comfort for many years. Now we will have to go through life recognising they will never come true, facing the sadness of psychic loss and finally coming to terms with reality. [8]

Working through our feelings

Most books on the subject of loss deal with only human death and dying. Yet there is no hierarchy of loss, we can't dictate or judge the intensity of our own or other people's feelings and to minimise, ridicule or try to ignore them just makes matters worse.

Our reactions to this situation vary, depending on our age, our life experience, our inner strength and outer support. Some of us can grieve privately and come through the process unharmed, but we all know people who are in denial, who harbour feelings of anger, resentment or self-pity, unable to come to terms with their loss.

The choices we can make include:

- Learning to grieve for what we lose throughout our lives can be viewed as a source of maturity and growth. It is not a completely negative process and it is one we will be going through many times, so it is important to find ways of coming to terms with loss.

- Everyone has feelings of loss over what other people may call 'small things'. Only you can know the depth of feeling this engenders, so you should never feel guilty or foolish.

- Don't push these feelings to the back of your mind. You will only be able to come to terms with loss if it is openly acknowledged (to yourself at least) and you have gone through a process of grieving.

- The process and rituals of mourning around bereavement are well defined and it is certainly worth reading up about the different stages of mourning, if only to see how others have dealt with a similar situation.

We can also choose to make a difference in our approach to other people's losses:

- Let people talk about the loss as much as they want.

- Listen to people when they grieve. You may have heard the same story before, you may find it all rather depressing and you may have problems of your own. But it is because nobody is really *hearing* their story or helping them to cope that people express the same ideas again and again. So listen to the best of your ability.

- Learn to recognise unspoken grief over any form of loss. Your friend's jokey reference to 'looking like Humpty Dumpty' may hide a lot of pain.

- You may find their situation quite ridiculous or trivial but it matters to them. Never belittle the loss.

- Gently remind people of why the loss occurred; the cat was very old, the old house was too expensive to keep up. People tend to forget the rational reasons for the loss and maybe blame themselves for being neglectful or making the wrong choice.

- Initially treat loss as seriously as if it were a bereavement, and then take your cue from the other person to make sure your expressions of sympathy correspond to their needs and not to your own.

Coming to terms with loss

Ultimately the real key to coming to terms with loss and moving on is to accept that we may never fully recover. Although it is our experience of the difficult side of life which makes us more interesting, empathetic and a fuller person, and although most 'emotionally intelligent' people do recognise that problems can enrich life, this may seem poor compensation for serious loss.

Feeling lonely

To remain healthy and contented in our later years we need someone to love, someone to talk to and something to look forward to. In our western society we often find ourselves alone, and loneliness (which is not at all the same thing) is both insidious and pervasive particularly as we grow older and friends and family dear to us die or move away. The chances are that almost all of us will be on our own at some point. Life lasts longer and relationships have become more complex; we change partners more often, or don't find a partner at all; we may not have a family, or may have lost touch with them; we are geographically more mobile and move away from our initial social circle; there are weaker neighbourhood links.

One of the pleasures of later life is having more 'personal space', whether that means taking a long walk in the hills, a leisurely bath or just a quiet moment before we go to bed. But finding ourselves alone in this sense, alone through choice and safe in the knowledge that there are people out there whom we can contact whenever we want, is very different from the powerful emotions involved when we are suddenly or unrelievedly by ourself. We may then feel overwhelmingly lonely.

Loneliness has little to do with the number of people we come into contact with and everything to do with a mental state of feeling bereft and isolated, useless, a state admirably described by the author Zoe Heller:

> People don't know what it's like to construct an entire weekend around a visit to the launderette or to sit in a darkened flat on Halloween night or to have the librarian smile pityingly and say 'goodness you're a quick reader!' when you bring back

seven books, read from cover to cover, a week after taking them out . . . I have sat on park benches and tubes and school-room chairs feeling the great store of unused objectless love sitting in my belly like a stone.[9]

New relationships

Before we reach extreme old age it is rare to find ourselves entirely on our own. We often have a network of, perhaps, weak relationships with former colleagues, an elderly relative, a neighbour. This is a good time to pick up one of those relationships, whether face to face, by letter, phone or through the Internet. If you don't have access to any form of social activity (perhaps you don't speak the local language, don't have any transport, are restricted by your own customs or family from going out on your own), what about by correspondence? Or volunteering your services?

The secret to forging new relationships in later life is diversity and acceptance of difference. It is unlikely we will find one group or one person who will fulfil all our needs at the same time. But maybe the choir we join will satisfy us partially, and chatting to a neighbour will fill in the rest. This is a very important point, we really have to make an effort now to meet a variety of people across the age and social spectrum each one of which will fill a social niche, but maybe none of whom will be a soulmate.

Nevertheless, feeling lonely is the scourge of our age and it would be unrealistic to say that it can be overcome easily, especially within the constraints of our later years but here are some suggestions that may help:

- Admit to yourself that you are lonely and assess how this came about.

- Do not blame yourself. Loneliness is the result of circumstance and not a defect in your personality.

- Loneliness is not inevitable, but changing things will require you to make some choices and take a few risks.

- Begin by eliminating the negative, avoiding situations that make you feel worse. One source of loneliness is comparison with others. You see everyone together in the shopping mall, couples in the cinema, in restaurants, such places increase your feelings of being on your own.

- Begin a correspondence through one of the many organisations which encourage people to write letters to prisoners, sponsored children or to lobby for a good cause.

- Use the Internet. Most of the suggestions on easing loneliness assume that we can get out to meet people, but increasingly the advice is to use the Internet. So if you are not yet using a computer, please refer to the Resources section and see if that is a possible solution for you.

- If you are socially shy and find it hard to make that first move, see if someone you know will go out with you. You will have to find the courage to say hello and introduce yourself but you have absolutely nothing to lose.

- Give yourself a treat. A small source of pleasure will get the adrenalin going which in turn will give you more energy.

- Reach out and talk to someone, anyone; socialising needs practice.

- Be a little less selective, do not expect that one person will meet all your emotional needs, accept contact wherever you can find it.

- Let down your defences just a little and respond positively whenever anyone contacts you.

- Think about having a pet. Pets provide a different form of friendship. A dog obliges you to go out and take a walk and is a pretext for striking up conversation with others. Its dependence on us makes us feel wanted.

- Consider setting up your own group to explore your interests. Put a notice in the local newspaper, supermarket, place of worship or library. There really are people like you out there. This is not as unrealistic as it may appear and you may be surprised at the response.

- Consider caring for others, perhaps through a volunteer group.

For further discussion of how to break your isolation and meet other people, look at the suggestions on page 195 under the heading 'Making new friends'.

Chapter 9

Spiritual life

···

I USE THE WORD 'SPIRITUAL' for want of a better. It comes with cultural baggage that may conjure up for some of us rather an exclusive world, putting us in a mental straight-jacket which prevents us from exploring dimensions beyond the tangible, material world. But 'spirituality', here in its widest most all-encompassing meaning, describes the opening of the mind to an increased consciousness of the world around us, a way of perceiving the interconnectedness of everything in the universe and our place in it, whether through the religious or the profane.

The ideal

Most of us recognise the benefits of a rich inner, spiritual life that can add depth and meaning to our existence. As time takes its toll and we find ourselves with less energy and less physically active, we can become more introspective and it is very rewarding to have the support of a dimension that can be reached whoever and wherever we are and in whatever circumstance.

> Getting older isn't easy for a lot of us. Neither is living, neither is dying. We struggle against the inevitable and we all suffer because of it. We have to find another way to look at the whole process of being born, growing old, changing and dying, some kind of perspective that might allow us to deal with what we perceive as the big obstacle without having to be dragged through the drama.
>
> Ram Dass[10]

Indeed many of us do not fear death so much as living a life that is somehow incomplete and purposeless. The assumption is often that when the pace of life becomes slower and we have more time for ourselves, we will concentrate more on this 'inner' life, and that as death approaches and friends and family disappear, our need to understand our place in the scheme of things will grow stronger. But while we may recognise the benefits, actually finding a spiritual dimension is more easily said than done; just hoping we will find ourselves with a meaningful inner life clearly isn't enough.

The dilemma of choice

Our parents' choice was either to continue the religious practice of their own parents, adopt a different faith or find themselves in spiritual limbo. For us today there is much greater knowledge and acceptance of alternative faiths, beliefs and practices and it is easier to find others who share our views, either face to face or in a 'virtual' community.

Many of us who were brought up in a faith do, indeed,

find that with more time for ourselves we can be increasingly active in our community and enjoy the sense of belonging and solace that our beliefs bring.

For people who believe, the satisfaction found in deepening religious practice is very satisfying. But for those of us who do not, or no longer believe, this satisfaction cannot be achieved through logic or rational thought. Never mind how much we want to believe, we just don't. If we were not believers or part of an organised religious community before reaching our later years, we are unlikely to join one now.

I was a science teacher and live my life very much in the rational world. I believe that religion is a crutch and wouldn't ever be able to accept anything that smacks of religion. However, I do envy the peace of mind and serenity that some of my friends have through their belief in a god.

Eric, 68

A fair proportion of us are not introspective, are not interested in finding 'hidden truths', and, like Eric, have an aversion to the whole idea of a supreme being and non-material matters. What many of us would like to find is a set of precepts for living which take us out of ourselves and which may, or may not, involve some form of organisation or meeting other like-minded people. Most of us want the peace of mind and tranquillity that comes through a sense of belonging and oneness with the environment.

There seems to be almost total unanimity that if we are aiming for satisfaction with our life as we grow older, this has to come from within ourselves and not from the outside. And, more importantly, that whatever path we choose to take to acquire inner peace and serenity, call it spiritual, contemplative or religious, it requires some effort.

It should be emphasised that this is not only achieved through organised religion, or even a belief in a supreme being; the concept of a spiritual dimension only requires that we believe there is some element in the world other than material. Call it what you will.

Contemplation, just quietly thinking about things, does not necessarily mean meditation; reminiscence – when we view our life and events – can be satisfying without putting our actions into a straightjacket of what is 'right' and 'wrong'. We can appreciate that some things are beyond the scope of understanding without having to accept the idea of a supreme being. We can develop our understanding of the interconnectedness of the world without believing in destiny or a special role for mankind.

But these are just words on the page and for those of us not in the habit of developing an inner/spiritual life, the whole idea may appear laudable yet somehow embarrassing and the goal unattainable.

Developing a spiritual life

So you may prefer not to begin this process and carry on as usual, or you may like to try some first steps towards developing an 'inner' life. There is no one way, 'quick fix' method, but here are some suggestions on how to begin a process that may at the outset not be entirely satisfactory, but which at least will set you on the right road:

- Browse the net or the shelves of your local bookstore. Read as much as you can and pick out those ideas that appeal to you without necessarily adopting an 'all or nothing' approach.

- If in the past you belonged to an organised religion, you will find comfort in returning, not necessarily to the beliefs, but to the rituals associated with them.

- Going to a familiar place of worship and listening to the prayers may bring back memories that are a comfort in themselves. Don't dwell on the faith you have lost, but on the beauty and comfort of things you recognise.

- Walk into places of worship of any faith, whether you are a member of that community or not. Usually these are areas or buildings of quiet and just sitting for a while is soothing and helps still the mind. It provides an ideal environment for thinking through problems and dealing with anxieties, quite irrespective of whether or not you practice that, or any, religion.

- You may want to join an interfaith group that explores questions of faith and God without being committed to one religious group or another.

- Consider the entire range of philosophical thought, such as Buddhism or Humanism, and not just those that you are familiar with.

Other ways to find peace of mind

If you would rather not join with others in exploring issues of spirituality there are many other ways you can find inner peace on your own:

- MIND, the mental health charity has listed the ten activities, which according to their research, bring the greatest comfort to the mind. So try to take up at least one of these. They are: music, gardening, writing, art, drama, poetry, walking, needlework, knitting and dancing.

- What these activities have in common is that they are deeply engrossing, give us an experience of total immersion and involvement and remove us from everyday problems.

- Take just one minute every day to think about what is important to you and see what you can do during the day to re-enforce your values.

- Make peace with yourself, releasing yourself from grudges towards life in general and certain people in particular.

- Increase the amount of time you spend being still, just allowing thoughts and ideas to wash through your mind. It can be standing by the window, out on a walk, waiting in the doctor's surgery or sitting on the bus. Take just a few moments to concentrate on the present moment.

- Use your senses to appreciate something that you find beautiful: music, chocolate cake, a lovely face, a flower, whatever gives you great pleasure and concentrate for a moment on that pleasure.

- Think through ethical and moral questions that you hear about through friends or the media and examine why you hold the views you do. What are the consequences of your conclusions?

- If you can go out to admire nature that's fine, but maybe you only have a potted plant, so see 'all the world in a grain of sand' and appreciate feelings of connectedness on a scale that is accessible to you.

- Direct your energy and attention inwards; listen to yourself and see how you really feel (not what you would like to feel, or should feel). Try to quieten the mind and trust your intuition.

Why seek a spiritual dimension?

There are no right or wrong answers in the search for spiritual life, and you need to explore this dimension at your own pace, in your own way and in your own time. You may want a community of like-minded people, the rites and rituals associated with organised faiths, or prefer private meditation and prayer, or just moments alone in quiet contemplation, or all or none of the above.

Ultimately the purpose of finding a spiritual dimension is that it helps us to live our *present* life. By giving us a sense of perspective, a greater awareness and a feeling that we are part of something bigger, or more forceful than ourselves, we gain the most positive attribute of all: that of greater wisdom and serenity.

Part 3

Our World

Introduction

···

THE WORLD IS CHANGING, people are changing, we are changing. What gives us a sense of security and well-being when faced with constant adjustments is the feeling that we are connected to people who care for and about us; people who provide us with practical and emotional support. The challenge of finding and maintaining a satisfactory social environment in our later years was by far the most pressing issue mentioned in the answers to my questionnaire.

The choices we make now concerning our social environment are different in nature from those we made in the past. Partly because our margin of error is reduced, and partly because they involve other people who themselves are changing in unpredictable ways. We may try to envisage our world over the next 20 or 30 years, but elderly parents, ageing friends, shifting family relationships, all mean that we have to weigh up our options carefully, reinforcing the social patterns and environment that contribute to our well-being. At the same time we eliminate, to the best of our ability and budget, those elements that we find less than satisfactory.

There is one important issue that I have not dealt with here which is the question of sex in later life, a subject, interestingly enough, mentioned to me only once. Much excellent material has been published on this topic and I have included a couple of titles in the Resources section.

The specific issues dealt with here are those that were given top priority by those I spoke to, mainly because so many of the choices in this area are life changing and hard to get right. There is no magic formula, but the options and suggestions presented should help to clarify complex questions.

Chapter 10

Our social networks

···

ALTHOUGH WE KNOW THAT all life means change, we are
still taken by surprise and get upset when friends and
family members, too, seem to change the rules of the game.
Increasingly and unpredictably, people come and go, bonds
strengthen and weaken. Only the very few of us who live in
small, tight-knit communities will be surrounded by the
same people at 75 as at 17. We still hope for permanence
although we know it is unrealistic to expect it.

> For many years I had a very close friend who was my main sup-
> port. Then she suddenly met someone at the age of 68 and
> went off to get married! To say I was devastated is an under-
> statement. I thought she would be there to the end.
>
> Gertie, in her seventies

At our age our expectations of life and of people are changing too – as are their expectations of us. We may become
more demanding, or more relaxed; find relationships easier
or more complex; develop a whole new social circle or

mourn the fact that so many people close to us are no longer around. We are made acutely aware that since change is the only constant, we can never take our social world for granted.

Our patterns of socialising inevitably evolve as we find it more tiring and stressful to travel great distances, visit under uncomfortable circumstances, eat food we don't much enjoy, mix with people who don't know us well and, what's more, are not interested in knowing us that well either. We become less tolerant of people's quirks and habits. Although we may have more time to socialise, sometimes we 'can't be bothered' to put ourselves out as much as before. This is a universally recognised characteristic of later life and is sometimes seen as proof that we are slowing down physically and becoming more rigid mentally. But this isn't really the case. After all, we do throw ourselves into new activities with great energy and, on the appropriate occasion, are very happy to get out the silverware and make a fuss – particularly if special friends or family members are involved.

Changing patterns

Instead, I believe we become more discerning in our socialising because the novelty factor has worn off and after, maybe, 40 years of a given activity, we just get less satisfaction from doing it yet again; putting on another four-course meal, travelling 60 kilometres (37 miles) to see an art show, or going to a drinks party where we don't know anybody. We've heard all Fred's stories several times before, put up with Jenny's excitable dogs all too often, had enough of chilly bathrooms or watching home videos. We have simply become very aware, in a way that was unthinkable before, of our own need to feel physically and psychologically comfortable, reassured, and to actually enjoy what we do. We are no longer willing to put ourselves into situations that we find boring, stressful or downright depressing. The 'obligation' side of socialising has gone. One of the greatest benefits of growing older is the joy of saying no.

Yet we have no desire to withdraw from the social world altogether. On the contrary, we are eager to meet new people who are like-minded and to maintain contact with friends and family. Our greatest fear is that our social world will disintegrate, yet there is a certain inevitability in this; people do die or move away, families grow up and get on with their own lives. We can only do our best to maximise the pleasure we get from our social world while we still can and – equally important but often overlooked – make sure that others enjoy us too.

> The most important thing to me is my friends. Without them I would be quite lost and I know that at my time of life maintaining a group of friends can be hard work. My family is far away and although I love them dearly it is those who are present that make my life as good as it is. They are not all people I would have chosen to be with when I was younger, but they are here for me now and make my life worthwhile.
>
> Michael, 80

Chapter 11

The family

···

IT MAY SEEM STRANGE TO begin a section on the family by talking first about *not* having family. But for once, those of you who, for whatever reason, do not have a family in any meaningful sense of the word, I think should have pride of place here.

Coping with the absence of family

You may have relations still living somewhere but are not in touch with them, or may not have a partner or children, or your relatives may all have died. Some of us in this position accept the situation with equanimity; we have become self-reliant and have built up a circle of friends to provide the support that others find, at least in part, through relatives. Others find it much harder to be on the outside of a family oriented world. People are so frequently defined, often quite irrelevantly, by their family relationships that it can be hard if we are not part of the system: 'Mother of five defies government order', 'Grandfather wins local marathon', and so on.

At a time when we take stock of our lives, assessing our achievements and our failures, it may be that the absence of a long-standing partner, children, or even grandchildren, is a source of sadness. You may be distressed that there is no one you will be able to turn to later on when you envisage that things may get tough.

> Lev and I have a son and daughter. Our son Roger married a woman much older than himself who cannot have children and our daughter is living with someone who refuses to have any. When we were younger we took this in our stride and didn't feel 'deprived' of grandchildren but Lev is now seriously depressed and I'm sure it's because there are no heirs, although Roger won't talk about it at all.
>
> Pat, 68

> I don't mind not having had a family but high days and holidays are a problem. There is such an emphasis then on family life and I feel completely excluded.
>
> Jack, in his seventies

Such feelings are not restricted just to those of us who have a very limited family or no family at all. Some of us may in fact have a family in theory but it is estranged, lives too far away or doesn't communicate, and in such cases we can feel equally distressed by society's emphasis on marriage, partnerships, children and grandchildren.

Perhaps you live in a community where status is entirely dependent on marriage and children and find yourself side-lined or viewed as less than whole, in which women are only given respect if they form one half of a partnership or are a mother, and men only if they have sons to carry on the line. You may have lived with this situation for a long time but as time goes by find yourself full of regrets. I have discussed this issue of past regrets more fully in Chapter 6.

As I said at the start of this book, there are many things we can't change in our lives but we can always choose how we react to a given situation. It isn't easy, it may require practice, but we can choose how we see ourselves within our environment. There may, indeed, be no compensation for lack of family, but we can take some steps to make life a little easier for ourselves.

If you miss having a family

Look at the following choices:

- Acknowledge your feelings and share them with someone, or an organisation, who will listen.

- Where appropriate, behave as though you were a relative to your friends' children and grandchildren. Being an honorary auntie or uncle is the next best thing.

- See if you can sponsor a child through a care agency.

- Try to stand in as parent, grandparent or godparent to someone, offering your services on a voluntary basis. There are organisations that need surrogate families.

- Don't be caught out at 'family' times. Make arrangements to be with friends, so that you're occupied or celebrating, too, in some form. Take some comfort from the fact that many holidays such as Christmas prove to be just too stressful for many who are choosing to spend them away from the family.

- Treat your friends extra well. You will come to rely on them more and more.

- Avoid those who do nothing but talk about their children and grandchildren or whose conversation excludes or belittles you.

- Avoid any activity or situation centred on the family that makes you feel uncomfortable or sad.

- If you have an heirloom or anything you would like to pass on to someone younger, either give it away now, (that way you are sure it will reach them and you can share in their pleasure) or make sure you are leaving it to them in your will.

- If you are good at carpentry, knitting, or any other handicraft, don't give up because there are no grandchildren to work for; make gifts for your local school, and so on.

We have a wonderful older lady who knits little toys to give to our young patients. When they are frightened or upset, we show them the cupboard shelf with the toys and they pick one out. It has worked wonders and we are really grateful.

Dental receptionist

If you have a friend with an absent family, or no family at all

Look at the following suggestions:

- Be careful when enthusing about your own family in front of them.

- Try to find common ground on subjects beyond the family.

- Include them in family occasions, if they would like this.

- Maybe give them an honorary family title such as 'uncle', if this is appropriate in your family and would be welcome to your friend.

- Encourage your children to treat them as a family member and to make a fuss of them when they come to visit.

- Make sure that you acknowledge their birthday and holidays with a card, telephone call, and so on.

- If you can see or feel that they are anxious about the future, see how you can help them.

- Encourage them to pass on a skill, family photos or a memento to someone in your family so that they know they will be remembered in the future.

- Emphasise how pleased you are to include them in your own social world.

The role of family in our lives: a realistic assessment

Even today when families exist in all sorts of weird and wonderful forms, and despite the debate about its influence and decline, the 'family' is still thought to be the most vital element in our social structure.

The trend towards looser and more diverse family structures began early in the twentieth century, but the greatest changes have occurred within our lifetimes. We may feel that many of those changes have taken place despite us, but in fact our own expectations and views on family have also evolved. Looking back at how our own parents interacted with their families we can see that we no longer feel the same degree of 'duty' and deference to older family members, are less dependent on the younger generation and enjoy far greater freedom to have a full social life outside the family.

Interestingly enough, when respondents replied to my question 'to what extent do you rely on the family for social support?', 75 per cent answered 'as little as possible', 'they are too far away', or 'not at all'. My sample was not statistically representative but it does show that a significant number of us does not believe, or no longer believe, that the family is/can be/should be, the primary source of help and support. This does not mean we are not intimately bound up with family only that our reciprocal roles and relationships have altered.

Families in the twenty-first century

With increased geographical mobility and expanding social opportunities, and with more active years ahead of us and more disposable income, we have far more lifestyle options than ever before. So, taking up the traditional role of family member and/or carer is only one choice among several – not only for us but for all family members across the generations. It is said that grandparents still provide most of the child care, and that in view of high house prices that there is an increasing trend for the generations to share a property, which may be true. But the fact of the matter is that in our later years most of us do not see ourselves primarily as child minders, nor do we have great expectations that the generations that follow us will offer their unstinting support. For most of us it is a balancing act. We want to be independent and we want other family members to be independent too, yet we want to be available to help out whenever necessary and hope that when we are in real need the family will be there for us as well.

The rituals

It is when the family all come together for special occasions that the nature of our relationships is brought into sharp focus. Family rituals can be fun; they give a sense of continuity and provide the milestones in our life. They are the regular occasions when the generations meet up, exchange news and readjust relationships before dispersing again, often for another 12 months. Some families only meet up at birthdays or funerals, others every weekend for a drink and a chat. Each family has its own way of doing things and has established patterns of behaviour specific to itself.

However, as we all know, sometimes these rituals are no fun at all. Either they never were fun to begin with, or, while the balance in the family has changed, the rituals have remained frozen in an unsuitable form: they are now a duty, something to be endured where everyone wishes they were somewhere else. Family visits, if they are for more than a day, can be tiring and yet, since many of us today live so far apart, it doesn't make sense to travel huge distances only to spend a few hours together. Inviting relatives to join us for a birthday or on holiday seems like a good idea at the time but may prove to be less than enjoyable. Even something as simple as an after-lunch stroll in the park, if it is a 'must do' event, can become a nightmare if no one really wants to do it any more and everyone goes through the motions only 'for old times' sake' or 'to please mum'.

Since most rituals are a carry-over from previous generations perhaps it is up to us, as the current torch-bearers, perhaps to do the family a favour and give some thought to these family functions. Should they continue as before, or be modified or abandoned?

> My son and his family got into the habit of coming to us every Sunday for lunch. It was wonderful to see the grandchildren week after week but meant a lot of work for me. I mentioned several times that perhaps we could go to their house, or out to a restaurant but somehow that never came about. Everyone loved coming to Gran's except Gran! I put up with it for too many years. I suppose I was frightened that if I said enough was enough, I wouldn't see the kids. Finally my husband was the one who called a halt. My son said a family tradition was broken but it wasn't a tradition that worked for me.
>
> Milly, 75

New families

If you would like to see a change there is a further point you should bear in mind. Relationships with our own children are not the same as with those who have married into, or are now part of, the family. They may be better or worse, but they will always be different. Anyone who is one half of a couple will be dealing with two lots of family occasions, which may make things quite stressful for them. Family jokes, family history, family habits can leave newcomers feeling bewildered, isolated, or just plain bored.

Things that annoy us

Taking as given that we love our family dearly (and even that may not be quite true) the most frequent family irritants that come to the fore whenever the entire family comes together will probably include some of the following:

- Diverging expectations of how you should treat each other; feeling there is either not enough or too much fuss being made.

- Being faced with unrealistic demands and expectations.

- Feeling you are in a straightjacket of duty, having to go through family rituals that have become meaningless.

- Putting up with reproaches, criticisms or unwanted advice.

- Having to hide the fact that you really don't like or get on with a family member, or in-law.

- Differing lifestyles, as highlighted around different sleeping and eating patterns (cooking, bedtimes, behaviour at table).

- Different tolerance levels of noise, tidiness, punctuality that make you feel like an intruder or intruded upon in your own home.

- Remaining on the sidelines, feeling bored and excluded while your partner has a wonderful time.

- Having to listen to the same stories over and over again, playing silly games or participating when you would rather read the paper.

- Being cast in a role you have long outgrown – the 'jokey uncle', the 'unambitious daughter', and so on.

What choices do we have?

> Whenever I ask my friends if they enjoyed their holiday with the grown-up family, they say 'it was wonderful but . . .' and then the conversation trails away as though they somehow feel ashamed of not enjoying the family 100 per cent. Am I in a minority of one when I say quite openly that family is a mixed pleasure?
>
> Mike, 59

We are at a time in our lives when we appreciate all the good things that the family can provide. But if your family has, as Mike says, become a mixed pleasure, what can you do to improve things?

The choices open to you will depend on the degree to which you rely on your family for support. If you feel they do not make a major contribution to your life then you have more scope for action than if you are anxious to remain on good terms with them all. It is futile to think that family members 'should understand my point of view'; the reality is that sometimes they do and sometimes they don't. If you wish to change the rules of family communication without too much upset, the art is to be able to gauge what the reaction might be. You can:

- Physically keep your distance, spacing out or shortening your visits. This will work only if your actions go unnoticed, or you can deal with the subsequent pressures or comments as well as possible feelings of guilt.

- Continue to be present on family occasions much as before but distance yourself emotionally, saying or participating as little as possible, *but* this can be very frustrating and ultimately denies you your rightful place.

- Try to change the 'rules of the game', in which case you need to express how you feel and establish more control over events. This may be very successful, or an absolute disaster depending on the extent to which the family has some insight and flexibility.

We always went to my brother's big country place for Christmas and it was really pretty tedious. I suggested that everyone come to me for a change, and then added that we could go to Mark's for Boxing Day. No one was very keen but the following year I said very quietly that I was spending Christmas in my own home, which was a tough decision. The following year, surprise surprise, they agreed to a change!

Rob, 59

- Accept that many family situations are not adaptable. People may be too set in their ways, not like or respect each other enough to want to compromise, be under financial, geographical or physical constraints. In which case gradually reduce the amount of time you spend or events you attend with them.

- Think through exactly what it is you would like to see happen and how it can be achieved. Assess carefully who it is that organises occasions, makes the decisions and controls the family before working out a strategy. Then think of ways to make the new state of affairs easier for this individual to accept.

- Avoid doing anything when you are upset or when arrangements have already been made. Wait until the next opportunity and act before, and not after, the event.

- Negative comments and criticism really don't help. Criticising from the sidelines is not a way forward, so always come up with positive alternatives. It is very hard for people to break family habits, particularly if they are seen as defining rituals that reinforce feelings of belonging. But realistic suggestions will usually get a hearing.

- Prevent yourself from sulking and appearing resentful. People can't know what you are thinking and feeling even if you think they should. It is amazing how surprised others are when we voice our feelings: 'How could I know?' 'I would never have guessed', and so on.

I hated attending the annual family barbecue with all the neighbours coming in and drinking too much. I decided to tell mum that I wouldn't be coming any more and she said she hated it too but that my dad loved these occasions. So I spoke to dad who said he only did it because mum loved showing off the garden! I tackled them both together and we all had a good laugh and never had another barbecue!

Terry, 60

The challenge of new family structures

Most of us growing up around the war years were part of that idealised household: married parents with two children, dog, cat and affordable house, possibly no car and certainly not more than one television, if that. The nearest we got to a stepmother was seeing Cinderella at the pantomime, and a stepfather was a character out of David Copperfield.

Family life has now changed beyond all recognition. For a start, only seven in ten of Britain's 17 million families include a married mother and father.[1] From time immemorial parent–child relationships have been intrinsically stressful; one generation tries to ensure that the next reflects and carries on its values, only to see the younger ones branch out on their own, rarely following exactly in parental footsteps except in the most traditional of societies.

But hard as it may have been before, for our generation things have got very complicated. Today we find ourselves surrounded by a myriad of serial partners, half-siblings, stepchildren, cross-cultural marriages, gay and straight domestic arrangements, with no set rules of social behaviour and no longer any norms against which to judge behaviour. In fact the very notion of judging anyone is now anathema. Every relationship is seen to be of equal value, an outlook that we may or may not share.

> Both our families came to our wedding and everyone got on really well. Within two years both sets of parents had divorced, and my mother had married my husband's father!
>
> Lee, 59

> My niece had a baby at 13, which really upset her mother and me but another sister who isn't married and has no kids, adopted her, which has worked out wonderfully well for everyone.
>
> Marie, in her sixties

The effect on us

It would be naïve and unrealistic to pretend that we all cope well with these fundamental changes in family patterns. We know that family life is changing but that doesn't mean we approve of it, can relax with it or don't have any comment we would like to make. Political correctness (or plain politeness) prevents us saying how we feel, yet being unable to express feelings of disapproval or sadness or just plain bewilderment, makes things even harder. Our feelings are storm-tossed, time and time again as we become attached to married or live-in partners, grandchildren and stepchildren only to see them exit, sometimes dramatically, from our lives.

Some of us have very strongly held ethical or religious views and believe that what we see is just plain 'wrong'. Yet to say as much is to invite trouble. At best we are seen as someone to be humoured, although we make everyone else uncomfortable; at worst, we're an intolerant leftover from a previous century whose views should be disregarded anyway.

So despite feeling upset and unhappy with these unfamiliar trends and combinations, particularly when they directly affect our own family life, we tend to put on a public face for fear of looking reactionary. We shrug and say 'I don't have much choice do I?' And the answer to that is: we may have more choice than we think.

What can we do?

I think my daughter is making a terrible mistake; she married just to have a baby but her husband provides no support either financially or emotionally and they are now barely on speaking terms. It is stupid for her to stay with him and bad for the baby. I would love to tell her to leave him but everyone says not to take sides although she's my daughter and I know she needs my support.

Gill, 66

Our son is gay and we have learned to come to terms with that. What we find much more difficult is the endless stream of partners. Our son has explained to us how the gay world functions but we feel uncomfortable and wish he would have a steady partner. We continue to welcome whoever he brings home, but don't like the set-up.

Geoff, 72

We can rarely influence our children's family arrangements once they have been made, which for them is perhaps just as well, but we can avoid making a distressing situation even worse. The points below are often emphasised by the professionals but aren't quite as easy to put into practice as they would have us believe.

On the assumption that you still hope to maintain a working relationship with your child, here are some suggestions on the choices you have:

- Say nothing. Nursing negative feelings on such an important issue is really hard but voicing your opinion can have far-reaching consequences.

- Come to terms with the fact that your children have to run their own lives.

- See yourself as part of the jigsaw that is their life and not as the centre of the family web. You may once have been the lynchpin, but you aren't any more, much as you may want to be. Your peace of mind and good relationship with your children depend on you accepting this fact. Your opinion now counts for less and that is exactly how it should be.

- Give up the notion of control. Although you still have a small degree of influence over your children, what you can do for them if they don't ask you for help is strictly limited. If they do ask for advice or help that is a different matter.

- Give up the need to know it all (*and* the need to say it all). There are large areas of your life which are a secret garden, so be generous enough to allow them private space as well.

- In trouble, support them first, advise later.

- Never give unsolicited advice and above all never take sides. Your views will come back to haunt you.

- If what you see makes you really unhappy, talk to your partner, to friends, or if need be to a counsellor but never to the people concerned, *nor to other family members*. This is important because talking to your siblings or to your other children divides their loyalties and is a sure way of your views getting back to those concerned.

- Ask yourself why, when you have not been asked, you are so keen to tell your children what you think. If you are telling yourself it is because you want them to avoid making or compounding a mistake remember the wise adage: 'Experience is a lantern that lights the path behind, but not ahead of us.'

- Your disapproval is highly unlikely to make your child

change the arrangement, so what exactly do you hope to achieve (apart from making youself feel a little better in the short term)?

- If the family arrangements make you so angry or uncomfortable that you choose to make a stand, for example by not inviting them into your home or taking them out of your will, you are perfectly entitled to do so, *but* don't believe it will influence your child's lifestyle. Be prepared as a result to face resentment and anger not only from your child but other family members too.

- Give some thought to what it is exactly that you so strongly disapprove of. Are you really upset by the arrangements or rather by what others may think?

Avoid cover-ups

If you are worried about the opinion of those around you (and your concern might be quite legitimate in your given community), don't try to cover up. It may take time for you to find the courage to talk about your child's living arrangements but at least any disapproval will be to your face and not whispered behind your back. And you may get a more sympathetic hearing than you think.

- If you have strong moral, ethical or religious views on family arrangements then none of the above apply. You will feel you have no choice but to speak out.

- Before you do say anything, however, think through the consequences of what you are doing; realise that your viewpoint might be quite incompatible with theirs and may lead to alienation and resentment. At least foresee this possible reaction and be prepared for it.

- Also realise that often your views are very well known to your child already. If they behave in a manner despite the knowledge that it upsets you, there is a deep-seated reason for it and they are unlikely to change their behaviour at this point.

- You can still tell them you love them and will give them all the support you can.

> My daughter lives with the son of a born-again Christian and they now have a baby. Ralph's mother genuinely believes her son and grandson are destined for hell unless her son marries but they have no intention of doing so. My daughter says that visits to her mother-in-law are becoming very fraught as she pressures them constantly to change the situation. I don't share her beliefs but I do feel desperately sorry for Ralph's mother.
>
> Dora, 67

One's heart goes out to the unhappy grandmother, whether we agree with her views or not. Jacqueline's situation is even sadder and all too frequent:

> My deepest regret in life is that I didn't really give our son and his partner a chance. Our community was very disapproving and we felt we had no choice. My husband wouldn't have either of them in the house and I went along with that. Now, when it's too late I wonder why I didn't make a stand. I loved my son very much but couldn't help him when he needed me. I'm just so angry with myself.
>
> Jacqueline, 78

Modern family arrangements are here to stay, at least for our lifetime, and when they concern our own children they can be hard to cope with. Even harder to accept, however, are the changes we face when there are grandchildren involved.

Chapter 12

Grandchildren and step-grandchildren

WE ALL KNOW THAT HAVING grandchildren can be more fun than having children. It is emotionally and financially easier, and because few of us are involved in the everyday strains and stresses of childrearing, we can relax with the grandchildren knowing that the responsibility lies not with us but with the parents. There is no single model for grandparenting and we are free to interact with them in whatever way we enjoy. We are there to give unconditional love and encouragement, to act as a bridge between the generations, to teach, listen, play, and, if our budget permits, to provide extras such as dance lessons or holiday pocket money.

A huge amount has been written on the subject of modern grandparenting not only because it has become an activity of middle rather than old age, but also to help with the hard-to-deal-with issues raised by the increasing number of single-parent and recomposed families. The shifting sands that are family relationships today have had a significant impact on the relationship between grandparents and grandchildren.

The effects of divorce

Children are the sad victims of divorce. So too are the parents, but grandparents who look on helplessly as domestic disputes unfurl and relationships disintegrate are victims too, their plight hardly recognised when the parents of their grandchildren fight, separate and reappear in a different domestic configuration. Thankfully there are now an increasing number of organisations that have taken up the cause of grandparents' rights, and the role of grandparents in this arena is gaining greater recognition.

Other problems

I mention several other problems below that preoccupy many of us and were frequently mentioned in my survey.

Stressful visits

You may feel that to admit that the recent visit of your son with his three young children was less than idyllic isn't quite acceptable. Confessing that you never liked babies, that toddlers distress you and that you find young children, or worse still, teenagers, very disruptive, is somehow seen as disloyal to the family. In particular if you come from a community that emphasises strong family bonds, negative comments can marginalise you or make you a figure of pity. So let's say it here: grandchildren can be wonderful, but at times they can also be a source of anxiety, annoyance and frustration.

We love our grandchildren dearly but find that we tire easily with them. They are active normal boys and expect us to be active with them. I'm not sure I really look forward to their visits any more, but hardly dare tell my wife, let alone my daughter.

Paul, 62

The success of visits with grandchildren varies enormously depending on whether or not they are accompanied by their parents. It is a universal truth confirmed by all the anecdotal evidence, that grandchildren are angelic on their own but diabolical when parents are around. Given this fact it makes sense to encourage grandchildren to visit on their own, also go out with them alone whenever we can or at least find recreational or quiet time with them away from mum and dad.

What can be done to minimise the stress? Here are some suggestions:

- Realise that you don't have to appear young and active. The grandchildren think you are ancient anyway, and their affection for you is not based on your ability to compete with the parents.

- Give your own needs as high a priority as those of the grandchildren.

- Avoid stressful situations to begin with; visits which are too long, too hurried, when the kids are tired, or there are too many other people around, or there are too many other things going on.

- See visits (to them, to you) as dedicated time. In other words forget about doing anything else but concentrating on the children. If not, you will be frustrated and the grandchildren will feel there is no 'room' for them. If you have more important things to do, shorten or rearrange the time.

- Discuss any (potential) difficulties openly with the parents.

- You alone can judge to what extent you can put up with the disruption, noise and fatigue. Yes, you can say no to visits, or decide when they should be.

We had planned to go on a cruise but at the last moment my son asked us to take the grandchildren while he was away on business. We didn't dare say no for fear we wouldn't be asked again. Silly of us really.

Graham, 57

- Stress often arises from grandchildren's boredom and even if you think that grandchildren today get bored far too quickly, the reality is that they do. You have to deal with very active children with short attention spans and not some idealised grandchild sitting quietly on the sofa or on your knee reading a book for a couple of hours.

- Make sure that there are things for them to do, perhaps make a list and let them choose, but also include 'down' time when they are expected to be on their own and you can get on with other things.

- Don't allow them to occupy all the adult space but do give them space to themselves. It may be a table for the jigsaw, some floor space to set out their toys or permission to use the computer. Make it clear that at the end of the day they have to clear their stuff away.

- Get them outside whenever possible; this gets rid of a lot of excess energy.

- When they've gone to bed, pour yourself a stiff drink or practise yoga or meditation!

Correcting bad behaviour

> I get on relatively well with my son-in-law but don't approve at all with the way he and my daughter bring up their children. They have no manners and show little respect. I feel sidelined but don't want to be the disapproving granny the whole time.
>
> Sally, 67

The issues of discipline, manners and the overload of material things come up time and time again. We know that grandchildren are naturally tiring and need a lot of care and attention, but our stress comes less from naughty behaviour (since we know full well that children can't be 'good' all the time) than from behaviour which we find distressing because it reflects a different way of raising children. Of course, our grandchildren are influenced in their behaviour by their parents, their peers, by what they hear and see on television. We are in no position to change the environment in which our grandchildren are brought up, and for our own peace of mind we do have to accept that society has different expectations of children today. But that doesn't mean we can't correct what we perceive as unacceptable behaviour, particularly if it occurs in our own home.

You have the following choices:

- If you see your grandchildren behaving badly in the presence of their parents, be careful before you step in to discipline them. That is the role (theoretically at least) of the parent. Bite your tongue and walk away if you get too annoyed.

- On your own you can be stricter or more indulgent as long as you never encourage anything which is forbidden at home.

- This implies that you have every right to set out your own 'house rules'. Children generally accept this without any problem as long as the rules are consistent and intelligible.

- There has to be some flexibility and you may have forgotten from your parenting days just how noisy and messy children can be. But if there is something that really makes you angry such as lack of manners and bad behaviour at table then you are perfectly within your rights to say so.

- If you think your house rules may upset the parents, inform them first but find the courage to be firm. If you don't say anything, you finish up like Sally, above, tense and resentful and dreading future visits.

- Remember that you will not be a good grandparent if you are in a permanent state of worry, annoyance or frustration.

- So that you are not perceived as a nagging granny or grandpa, give praise as often as you express disapproval.

- Don't make a big issue out of things that you know will lead to trouble. Forget the broccoli, set bedtimes, television restrictions. Provided you are not going against the fundamental principles of the parents, you should do whatever it takes to make life as easy as possible for yourself.

Step-grandchildren

This section relates to both your children's stepdaughters and sons, or your own stepchildren's offspring.

> We invited our daughter to come and spend a few days with us by the sea. Naturally we included her partner and stepson in the invitation but were quite upset when she asked if her partner's other two children who live with their mother could come too. How could we say no? We had hoped to have moments alone with our daughter but the visit was exhausting and we didn't enjoy it that much.
>
> Nick, 72

> When I set up home with Mike, I didn't quite realise what was involved in taking on his three adult children, their partners and a half a dozen grandchildren. I have my own family that I want to see and it is hard to fit everyone in. There are problems of logistics but also of cost. And I feel emotionally on a roller coaster.
>
> Ann, 64

The recomposed family

When we become part of a recomposed family either through our own change of partner or our children's, we find ourselves in uncharted waters. There is genuine ambiguity about the extent to which stepchildren and in-laws are, or can become, an integral part of our own family. Some of us have no problem in drawing them into the family circle without any distinction. But we may find that the arrival of newcomers is an intrusion. If we find them difficult to handle, unresponsive or unappealing in any way, we have trouble maintaining a decent, let alone good, relationship with them.

Do we have to see everyone at the same time? Can we have special moments apart with those we are directly related to? Should gifts and love and attention be divided equally between them all? Can we in some way privilege those we feel are really 'ours'? Just how far does a recomposed family stretch? Are four sets of grandparents now part of the equation, and what if they themselves are remarried? The possible permutations are simply endless, and provide a rich terrain for new and exciting relationships as much as for frustration and conflict.

Getting along

There are lots of questions and no easy answers. Each family chooses its own arrangements and the choices, which may be excellent for one family, may be quite inappropriate for another. But the issue of step-grandchildren isn't one which will go away and the dilemmas facing Ann and Nick are common ones.

Points to ponder:

- Unless you are Superman or Mary Poppins, you will inevitably have difficult moments with the stepfamily. The situation is intrinsically flawed. You will have been talked about even before they meet you, and you will step into a situation with all sorts of preconceived and prejudged feelings floating around that have little to do with the real you. If the new family likes you, that's wonderful, but if they don't, it doesn't matter. It is not a popularity contest so don't take things personally. All step-parents and step-grandparents are in a really tough position.

- Obviously it is best to discuss things openly with your partner, but there are inevitable tensions that can make this quite hard to do, particularly if you don't particularly like or approve of your stepfamily and grandchildren, yet know it's unwise to say so.

- In all families, some members are more accessible than others. But try to divide high days and holidays fairly between them all.

- How often you see your children is a separate issue from how often you see your stepchildren. In theory one should not depend on the other but realistically, since time and money are limited, there may be some hard choices to make.

- Suggest and encourage your partner to see the other family on their own sometimes. The stepfamily may well prefer that too.

- Don't criticise step-grandchildren as you put your partner in a difficult situation, but don't keep your feelings to yourself. The choices involved are hard to make, but have to involve you both. Unilateral action may be a choice, but should only be the last resort.

- If you begin to resent their intrusion in your life suggest that there should be more sharing of the chores, you go out more often for meals, or go away yourself for part of the time that they come to visit.

- Make sure that you appear scrupulously fair in the treatment of stepchildren; they are very susceptible to the question of favouritism.

- Respect the other family's traditions whatever the cost to you. Don't belittle or criticise them but expect the same behaviour from them too.

- Naturally, you want an opportunity to favour your own family, but it should be done out of sight of the others. It is important that occasionally you find yourself alone with your own children and grandchildren, and you will need to plan these occasions carefully.

- Remember that they have other grandparents and other family obligations. Their lives as well as yours are very complicated emotionally and practically. The situation calls for patience and co-operation on all sides.

- If you feel you can't win, however hard you try, do what makes you, and hopefully your partner too, feel comfortable and so at least you will please yourself.

Grandparenting from a distance

The issue facing many of us is this: if we live a long way away from our grandchildren, and perhaps can count on our fingers how often we will see them in the future, just how much effort should we make to keep in contact with them; is it worth it, for them, for us?

We used to live very near our grandchildren and since both parents were working, we would pick them up from school and look after them in the holidays. They were an absolute delight and there is no doubt they gave us a new lease of life. Now they have moved away and we're not sure things can be the same, we try not to get too upset but there is a hole in our life now.

Robin, 75

Our son divorced and his ex-wife remarried and moved a six-hour car journey away. Our son always brings the children to see us but what we are finding really hard is that the children's mother is rigid about the timetable and doesn't allow us to talk to them on the phone. The visits have become very strained and upsetting. We often feel like giving up. We don't know what to do for the best.

Pierre and Jo, in their late fifties

Many of us today are separated by distances that make everyday grandparenting out of the question, and this has a huge impact on the relationship with grandchildren. We are all thinking of ways to be effective grandparents without frequent one-to-one contact and the detailed sharing of daily life. We may decide, for any number of reasons, that we are more comfortable not trying to establish or maintain a relationship at a distance, not least of all because we get no encouragement or co-operation from the parents. And you may have other things in your life that compensate, or other more accessible grandchildren. But even if we don't see grandchildren all that often, that doesn't mean we don't have a very important role to play, and to give up on this relationship or feel that 'out of sight is out of mind' is to deprive ourselves of a link that can still be very fulfilling for both sides, even if we are not present very often.

The value of grandparents

All children love having adults take an interest in their lives, and the parents of their parents provide a vital link with the past, with the wider family network. We all remember our grandparents whether they were near or far, nice to us or not. I didn't see my own grandmother from one year to the next but she sent regular letters, gifts of chocolate or clothing, which I remember very vividly and loved receiving; and this certainly created a bond.

If you are pining for a close relationship with your grandchildren, make sure that you are doing everything you can to be in contact with them and don't underestimate your influence on their lives even from a distance. With appropriate communication and a little effort we can play a significant part in our grandchildren's lives and they in ours, so that on those occasions when we do meet up it becomes a very special event.

In many ways our lives are more complex than those of our parents, but in one respect it has been made considerably easier. Modern technology has given us a welcome helping hand in bridging the miles and nowhere is this so valuable as when strengthening ties with distant grandchildren. The most important thing is to maintain a form of communication, appropriate to their age and one they enjoy using (don't expect grandchildren to write letters just because you do, but they might send you a drawing or email).

When we choose to bond at a distance

The following ideas can help to strengthen the bond:

- Talk things over with the parents to make sure that you call at the right time. Don't send inappropriate gifts or make suggestions that go against parental wishes or rules.

- When grandchildren are old enough, use the telephone whenever you can. Make sure you speak to all grandchildren in turn and whenever possible out of earshot of the parents. Encourage them to call you too.

- Send them photos, newspaper cuttings, or paper stick-ons. All children love getting things in the post with their name on it.

- Show that you take an interest in their friends, how they are doing in school, in the details of their life. It is wise to write down what they tell you because you are unlikely to remember the name of their school friends or the latest video game.

- Talk to them about their parent when he or she was a child; they love hearing stories about when their parents were young.

- Take lots of photos with a digital camera and send them via email. They have a wonderful immediacy and speak louder than words.

- Send them personal postcards or mementos of any trip you make, and small things you find such as a pretty feather or seashell.

- Make small gifts. Anything made by granddad or gran is infinitely more precious than something bought in a store.

- Share their life but also tell them about yours. The learning is a two-way process.

- Send them family things, maybe a baby spoon or photo of great-great granny which will give them a sense of connection. But make sure all grandchildren get something in turn.

- Get them involved in doing something with you that you both like and help them build up their interest. A recent television programme interviewed young collectors who had, by the age of 11 or 12, already become experts in their specialist field (model steam engines, miniature cups and saucers, porcelain figurines, and so on). Almost without exception they said their enthusiasm had been triggered by a grandparent.[2] This is something that can easily be done at a distance.

- Time any visits to coincide with special occasions, either a religious festival you celebrate, a birthday or when they are in the school play.

Distance grandparenting is not the same as living next door, but it need not be of less worth, nor should we ever underestimate its importance to the grandchildren. It requires effort and creativity but it can become a unique and irreplaceable element in our social world, which carries us confidently into the future.

Chapter 13

Elderly family members

···

W E ARE THE SANDWICH GENERATION, caught between our children who become independent much later than we did and the dependency of our parents who live well into their eighties, nineties or even to be over 100. Although we may have new freedom on retirement, we may also have the constraint of looking after the seriously old for what can be a considerable period of time. It has been calculated that the average woman spends as many, or more, years assisting in the care of one or both of her parents as she did in caring for her children.[3]

Few of us have to shoulder the task of caring for the very old entirely alone and luckily there are now many sources of advice and everyday help. However, the practical side of caring, while important and time-consuming, seems to be less of an issue for most of us than the conflicting emotions and psychological pressures involved. Although dealing with parents in extreme old age can be rewarding, it can also upset us emotionally and disturb our domestic equilibrium.

I found it an enriching and rewarding experience to take care of my uncle. He was great fun, never complained and made a huge contribution to our family.

Roger, 60

I never got on with my mother even before she got really old and crotchety. Things have gone from bad to worse and it takes huge reserves of patience for me to be able to deal with her at all.

Barbara, in her early sixties

It's a privilege to be able to repay, with love and care, some of the debt that we owe our parents.

Sandra, 73

Emotional dependency

When someone we love, or feel responsible for, becomes dependent it is often easier to deal with their physical needs than to provide emotional support. Adapting a home, finding residential care, providing the appropriate services may take up our time and energy. But it is somehow less stressful than having to deal with the psychological burden which forces us to review our relationship with the person involved in ways that we may not be comfortable with, or which we find emotionally draining.

The situation is relatively straightforward when we are asked directly for help. It's far more difficult when it becomes obvious to us that help is needed but is not being asked for, or is being refused. A suggestion on our part that we know for sure would enhance someone's quality of life can become a source of drama or reproach. There is hardly a family that hasn't gone through this intermediate period, when an elderly relative who is either unaware of their own situation, or aware but frightened of change, adamantly refuses what we regard as a definite 'improvement'. It could be the use of a walking frame, an emergency call system or quite simply accepting home help.

The real challenge is that although the very old may behave like children and be as demanding as children, they aren't children. They cannot and should not be treated as such, yet it is all too easy for us, after innumerable discussions that have led nowhere or resulted in recriminations and frustration on all sides, to take a short cut and decide things for them. This leads to even greater frustration on their part and further complaints either from them or even from other members of the family. Striking a balance between what the elderly want, or say they want, and a realistic course of action is time consuming and saps our energy. And if we are the person who has taken on most of the care responsibility, it is easy to brush aside the opinions of other siblings or concerned friends whom we feel aren't fully aware of the problems or don't have the same everyday contact.

My brother has no idea what is involved in looking after father, he's full of flippant suggestions that can't possibly work.

Marina, 70

Every time I come to see mum the neighbour pops over to tell me everything that's going wrong; I don't know what she hopes to achieve by doing this, she just annoys me – as though I didn't know what's happening.

Stan, 63

Without any doubt and whatever the circumstances, when we take responsibility for an elderly person, whether alone or as a shared task, it has a profound effect on our lives. It may be for the good: strengthening family ties, bringing us closer to a beloved parent, feeling the satisfaction of repaying them now for what they have given us in the past. We may enjoy the quiet moments spent with an older person in reflection and reminiscence. On the other hand we may be caring for someone we don't much like, who is ill-tempered, demanding and not very good company, or who presents us with physical and psychological problems we feel we are not equipped to deal with.

Whatever the circumstances, this is a new aspect to our lives and one that will preoccupy us both physically and mentally. It can have a profound impact not only on our own lives but also affect all the relationships around us – first and foremost that with our partner whose support we will need, and subsequently with friends and other family members too.

> Mother living with us had had more impact on my relationship with my partner than I thought possible. With my friends as well, I can see they feel obliged to include mum in the conversation when they visit and not all of them are comfortable with that.
>
> Kim, 55

In today's world of recomposed families the links between family members are often weaker or of a different nature than before. A new partner may not have the same emotional attachment to our family or old friends as do partners of long standing. As a result, finding support during this period may be more difficult.

I have a good relationship with my second husband, Alan, but when mother got Alzheimer's I realised I was on my own. I got little help from the family, the kids didn't visit her even when she could still recognise them and Alan was always too busy to pay a visit. I had a job, family and total responsibility for my mother. If I'm honest I would say that it altered how I feel about Alan; in my time of need, he just wasn't there – whatever reason he may have had for not helping out.

Teri, 65

Understanding an elderly person's needs

The following are some suggestions to make things easier for the elderly (and indirectly for you, too, because if the elderly feel more at ease they will relieve the pressure on you):

- Remember that listening is action. Give them enough time to talk and explore their concerns and grievances, memories and emotions.

- Concentrate fully on them and what they say, but for shorter, more frequent, periods if possible.

- Give every reassurance but be cautious with suggestions. They have probably heard your advice before and won't take any notice. It is upsetting for them to hear what they should be doing and it's frustrating for you.

- Think hard whether the suggestions you make aren't more for your own comfort than for theirs.

- However, you are also part of the equation and arrangements must take into account your needs as well as theirs.

- Allow them to talk about death and dying if they want to. If they say, 'I have nothing to live for any more', respond with, 'So tell me about it.'

- Listen to what they're saying beyond the words. All too often their frustration, anxiety or aggression focuses on something quite irrelevant, and no amount of dealing with the small issues will resolve the fundamental, underlying problem.

- Ask yourself if it is at all possible to do or provide what they ask. Or are their requests unrealistic?

- If they are unrealistic, think how best to make them realise that their request is impossible; could someone else do this better than you? Is there a compromise you can suggest? Or can you offer to try out an unrealistic plan, knowing what its outcome will be, but allowing them to come to this conclusion themselves?

- Slow down both in speech and action. It is frustrating to have to repeat things ten times over, but, deafness apart, it just takes a longer time for the elderly to absorb what is being said. As their sense of time diminishes and there is greater memory loss, find the necessary patience. Avoid phrases such as 'I told you that yesterday' or 'surely you remember', because they obviously don't.

- Try to give them a modicum of control in some area of their life. Include them in decisions as much as possible, ask them what they would like you to do or what they suggest rather than presenting them immediately with solutions.

- Give them a routine; call on the same days at the same time. This prevents them worrying about when you will contact them and they have something to look forward to.

- Try to steer the conversation towards subjects of general interest, the latest news, the weather, and so on. This way the conversation does not revolve around only them. It also pre-empts discussion of what more you should be doing for them and everything that is going wrong.

- If you do not see them regularly, send small gifts or flowers or something that shows you are thinking of them.

Helping yourself

The following suggestions are aimed at making life easier for you, because you matter too:

- Develop a sense of proportion. Provided the elderly are warm, safe, well-fed and receive adequate medical care it really doesn't matter if the cupboard isn't too clean, if they are getting enough exercise or if they are eating too many sweets, and so on. They are at the end of their lives and ultimately social conventions are irrelevant.

- Try to gain a sense of perspective. We are very much bound up emotionally with those close to us but if they become too demanding, insulting or manipulative, we need to take a step back. If we do not maintain our own mental equilibrium we can't possibly hope to be of help to them.

- Get rid of the guilt (see below).

- Realise your limits. The elderly person may not control his or her environment but neither do you. Nor will you be able to change a behaviour pattern established decades ago.

- Save your breath and don't push ideas which obviously are not acceptable to them.

- Don't allow yourself to be swamped by anxieties concerning the unknown future. You can't know how long someone will live, how events will unfold, or what form your responsibilities will take.

- Do your best, but only as far as you are able to. Do not allow caring for or about someone be at the expense of other relationships.

- Treat yourself extra well during this period; do whatever makes you feel good and gives you pleasure.

- Keep extra activities, responsibilities and commitments to a minimum. You can pick them up again later. Coping with a very elderly person is extremely tiring both mentally and physically. It can't just be 'fitted in' with the schedule you had before.

Having a parent live with you

Be under no illusions, having a parent live with you is a 24-hour-a-day, 365-days-a-year job. It is a tough assignment even if you have always got on well together and there are no serious health problems.

You may think you are the only one that cares enough, has a big enough house and enough time or money to take responsibility for a parent. You are making the assumption that your parent cannot be looked after by anyone else inside or outside the family, and this assumption will be the basis for any decisions you make.

Although we need to differentiate between caring for a parent during a terminal illness and looking after someone who is very old over a period of five or ten years or more, even in the best of circumstances this choice will cause a major upheaval in your life. There will be constant physical and emotional demands and undoubtedly some sacrifices will have to be made.

> I didn't have a minute's hesitation in looking after Mum when she was terminally ill. In fact she was with us for a couple of years and during that time I had her to myself and we had some wonderful moments.
>
> Emily, 61

> When Dad moved in with us, I quickly realised that he wasn't in any state to be looked after at home but by then it was too late. It's dreadful to say but luckily for him he died after a year with us, a year which was stressful beyond belief.
>
> Penny, in her late fifties

So when considering the options it is important not to act on the spur of the moment or out of pity, anger or desperation. Above all you need to consult other family members fully before making changes which will have a profound effect on all your lives. You need to be highly motivated and your degree of motivation has to be shared by other members of the household and, above all, by your partner.

Here are some good reasons to choose to look after someone in your home:

- You love your parent very much and want to be with them at the end of their life.

- You are living alone or are under-occupied and relish the idea of having someone to look after or another presence in your home.

- You are a caring professional and want to extend your skills to someone dear to you.

- You feel a duty towards your parent which you want, and feel able, to fulfil.

Mum and I were very close and when she had a stroke and I retired we both found great comfort in each other's company right up to the end of her life. She was my best friend and I miss her dreadfully.

Dina, 67

And here are some bad reasons:

- Acting out of a sense of duty.

- Acting out of a sense of guilt.

- Acting under pressure from other family members, friends or care professionals.

- Acting without a clear enough sense of the demands it will make on you and others in your household.

- Going against the advice or wishes of your partner or other members of the household.

- Taking on this new responsibility when there are obvious physical, financial or emotional constraints.

In these cases your motivation will not be strong enough to carry you through the tough times and will lead to tension and acrimony. It may even leave you with a sense of grievance for the rest of your life.

> I agreed that Sally should have her very frail father come to live with us but to be honest we had no idea what was involved. Sally is always tense and I can see she has to juggle our needs as a couple with his needs, and it isn't easy. We have only been married five years and have had to make a lot of adjustments with our respective children, and now this. It has had a negative impact on our relationship and although we do discuss it, we don't seem to make any progress.
>
> Stuart, 69

Feeling guilty

> Never mind what I do for my mother, she grumbles. I lean over backwards but she still makes me feel guilty.
>
> Robin, 70

> My parents never complain but I feel I'm not doing enough for them. They aren't happy as they reach extreme old age and to be honest I don't know what would help but I still feel I'm the one who should find the solutions for them.
>
> Bruce, 60

> I'm told by everyone, including the family doctor, that if I don't do everything I can to help my parents now, I will feel really bad later on. But how much is enough?
>
> Marcia, 63

The most frequent comment when it comes to caring for the very elderly is 'I somehow feel guilty'. This sense of having a bad conscience does not seem to be in proportion to the amount of help, love or care we have, or have not, given the person. It is induced either by the social group in which we live or by the elderly person, a sibling or someone else close to us who thinks that we should be doing, or should have done, more.

Feelings of guilt are a cultural phenomenon and some cultures, more than others, regulate family relationships by fostering this sense of guilt. Guilt is a form of social control instilled in childhood and brought to the surface whenever important issues involving family or relationships are involved.

> The kids are great with their grandparents and don't really understand why I have such difficulty in finding enough patience to deal with them. They make all sorts of indirect comments. But of course my parents don't treat the children as they treat me; they say I am the wicked witch but I feel like Cinderella!
>
> Sheryl, 62

From the frequent but insidious phrase, 'I was wondering when you would call me again', to the blatant, 'what did I do to you that you're treating me this way now?', or just, 'don't you think you should …' we instantly have the childhood reflex of feeling obliged to please. When friends or family make us feel guilty in this way, we may be stirred to action, but it also engenders a degree of resentment that can make it even harder to do what others expect of us.

How to feel less guilty

It's hard to lose the feeling of guilt altogether but you can reduce it. The following suggestions might help:

- It is normal to feel some guilt for we can rarely, if ever, live up to others' expectations.

- Take time to reflect on who or what exactly is making you feel guilty.

- If others are making you feel bad, remember they are only pressing a lever which is already in place.

- Ask yourself if there is any truth in the reproaches? Or are the pressures on you incessant and truly unreasonable?

- If they are, are you able to pre-empt or circumvent them? Can you go any way at all to meet some of the demands comfortably, so as to avoid others?

- Imagine if you were able to concede to the demands; would this be the end of the matter? Or has it become an automatic behaviour pattern that would continue anyway?

- If there are material reasons (distance, money, your own state of health) why you can't respond to the person's wishes, make sure you have explained these reasons clearly to everyone involved, *but* don't expect them to agree with you – they have a different agenda.

- Find someone to talk to about how you feel. It's a great relief to share your thoughts and experiences.

- Guilt is a power play, often used as a last resort. Feelings of powerlessness are being transferred to you by another person, and if you can empower the person in some small area this may be enough for them to take the pressure off you.

- If the guilt is coming from a sibling, ask them frankly what they would want, and what they are prepared to do. It may be that they are projecting their own sense of guilt on to you to relieve their own burden. Try to share that burden.

- Tell yourself that you are not responsible for the situation in which the person making you feel guilty finds themselves, although they may say you are.

- Accept that you cannot live their lives for them. The responsibility for the situation they find themselves in has to be shared.

Care and the wider family

Taking responsibility for dependent or semi-dependent parents, or any elderly friend or relative involves not just us and them, but also our entire family and social network.

The friction in families over the care of elderly parents is second only to that over inheritance, bringing into sharp focus, as it does, the exact nature of all our family relationships. If yours has been a close family in the past, it will continue to be so, and the care of your parents can strengthen the bond between you all as you live through the inevitable joys and upsets. But if there has been latent or open friction or even just poor communication over the years, this will come to the surface again now.

I lived in the same area as my mother but my brother had moved away, so it was quite normal that I should see more of my mother than he did. He got on well with her when he did visit and so when I retired we all decided together that mother and I would move nearer to my brother so that he could see my mother more often and perhaps share the responsibility of looking after her when she was no longer independent. However, we now live just ten minutes away from his family and he doesn't visit any more than before. He always has a reason why he can't come across and neither he nor the grandchildren make much effort. What is distressing is that my mother is upset. I don't have children and she was really looking forward to a richer family life.

Rosemary, 62

Rosemary's is the most frequent complaint: others aren't assuming their fair share of the burden, they don't call often enough, visit enough or help enough.

You may have taken on the major responsibility of looking after your parent quite naturally and be more than happy to continue looking after them, but just because you've taken this on yourself does not mean that other family members will do so as well. Exploring their past relationships with your parent may give some insight as to why they are not helping more and there may be genuinely valid reasons.

On the other hand they may indeed be thoughtless, selfish or feeling so guilty they prefer to avoid the situation altogether. But unless your family broke up a long time ago and relationships have collapsed beyond repair, you are quite right to feel that the responsibility should be shared – even if this remains only a hope. All you can do is to assess the situation as realistically as possible, act on your conclusions and if the outcome is not as you wish, come to accept that the situation is beyond your control.

If you are the person with the most responsibility and feel, like Rosemary, that you are not getting enough support or that the help is inappropriate, before choosing a course of action consider the following points:

- If siblings are involved, you won't change their behaviour. It is far too late – if it were ever possible – so you can only change how you view and deal with the situation; lower your expectations of help from them.

- Do not expect others to assess the situation in the same way as you. You may be the only person who has an overall, comprehensive view of what is going on. Or you may be missing something that's clear to others.

- Ask them for advice and their opinion. Refuse to make important decisions on your own; if you do not trust your judgement and feel you may have to explain your decisions at a later date, either to yourself or someone else, make a record of what you are doing or giving. This may be important when misunderstandings arise, you have to justify your actions or there are questions of inheritance or taxation.

- Do not expect any recognition or reward; if you get it, it will be a bonus but you must be prepared to do this for yourself and your parent, not for anyone else. And forget about gratitude. The family may indeed be thankful, but may also think you are doing this because it's easier for you than for them.

- If your parent is upset about other family members, don't reinforce that feeling, however much you may agree with their comments. Remain neutral and do what you can to strengthen the contact behind the scenes. If it doesn't happen, it isn't your fault. Pass on, very clearly, any requests coming from your parent.

- Tell others explicitly what help you would like from them and also what you intend to do.

- Inform them of any costs involved.

- Tell them when you are angry about something but do your best not to bear a grudge against other family members who are not helping out; accept that this is the way they are for your own peace of mind.

- Inform the family about what is happening whether by phone, email or letter. Don't minimise the difficulties and appear as though you are coping when you aren't but don't only complain. Talk about the brighter moments too.

If you are the 'absent' sibling

There are probably very good reasons why you are not able to look after an elderly person in the way that you would wish or that others think you should. If distance is the issue, the cost and time involved may make for infrequent but emotionally charged visits; in a crisis the price and complications of the journey may make it hard to decide when to come or whether to come at all.

> I know my sister has taken on the task of main carer for father. I live a long way away but come as often as I can. Father never

has any reproaches but I can feel the resentment in my sister although I am really doing my best.

Fred, 62

The following suggestions might ease the situation:

- Give recognition to the main carer. You may feel relieved of responsibility because the person lives in the family home but doesn't have a family themselves, has more money, is the beneficiary of the will, appears to be coping very well, offered to take the job on in the first place, and so on. But whatever the reasons, they are doing something that you can't or won't do. And it's a very tough job, so give credit where it's due.

- If they are doing more than you, quite simply say thank you. This defuses the situation and minimises recriminations either during the care period, or afterwards.

- Ask for news regularly.

- Ask frequently what you can do to help even if you know the answer is 'not much'.

- Explain clearly that you are doing everything you can and if you feel guilty because you can't do more, say so.

- Don't allow your parent to suffer because you have problems with other family members.

- Talk to your parent or contact them at every available opportunity.

- Make sure the carer isn't neglected by others, or isn't neglecting other relationships.

- Be prepared to listen to some grumbling and reproaches; the person looking after your parents needs to sometimes let off steam.

My brother-in-law felt very guilty about not being able to help with my mother-in-law's care. He has to travel a lot for his work and doesn't have much money or the chance to come to see her regularly. Last year when he was here he invited all the family to a very expensive meal in the best restaurant in town and my husband thought it was a complete waste of time and money. But I told him to take it for what it was, a way of saying thank you to those of us who are able to care for his mother and to show that although he is absent, he is still part of the family.

Kristin, 67

The above may make sense in theory, but the fact is that when it comes to dealing with elderly family members, what we do or say, how much help we give or can expect is determined by the past far more than in response to the present. Our choices will be heavily influenced by the degree of support we get and that, in turn, depends on the nature of our past relationships that can't be easily disregarded or modified.

Chapter 14

Friends: old and new

··

HAVING A NETWORK OF GOOD, supportive friends is important at any age but in our later years it becomes vital and is certainly one of the keys to successful ageing. Whereas in some communities family is paramount and irreplaceable, for some of us our friends play an equal or even a greater role in our lives than family.

The importance of friends

A small circle of reliable friends is much better than many who can't help you out.

Don, 71

My friends here have saved me from madness.

Judy, 75

It is now that we have more time to socialise, when younger members of the family have grown up and are no longer around so much, when some of our friends have already died or are seriously ill, when we have moved to a new area, or our friends themselves are on the move, that we tend to think more than before about friendship and what it means to us. We are sometimes surprised to see just how much our social world can change and how our friendships evolve.

As Maryanne Vandervelde, an expert on retirement, explains in her book,[4] many people think of their colleagues at work as friends and are shocked after retirement when they learn that this just isn't so. There may be social rejection or confusing signals from those you had previously spent a significant part of your life with. As we become conscious of the shift in our social circle, we either accept this as inevitable and concentrate on those friends we do have or make an active effort to expand our social network, even in the knowledge that old friends are irreplaceable. Growing older surrounded by a warm circle of friends is everyone's dream but can be difficult to achieve.

As we think about our social circle we become more aware of our need for contact with people who are geographically accessible. Wonderful though it is to have friends throughout the world, when we would like a quick chat, to see a friendly face, have someone to share a meal or the shopping with, this is only possible with someone close at hand. As our mental and physical energy lessens, even if only slightly, it is a comfort to meet up with friends whose visits do not require a lot of travel time or preparation.

I was rather taken aback when a friend who lives nearby said to me the other day that the reason she enjoyed my company so much was because I lived 10 minutes away! I would have preferred her to say it was because she liked my company but I take her point that it is our nearness that makes the contact easy.

Mary, 69

Over time the number of friends we have may alter, and so too may the nature of our friendships. We place increasing value on 'good' friends and become more uncomfortable with 'poor' friends. Some of us take having, or not having, friends for granted but others feel it worthwhile to make some effort in this direction and wonder what choices are open to us.

Being a good friend

We give a great deal of thought to what we look for in a friend but not always enough to being that good friend ourselves. Throughout life we've known that being a good friend means giving more than receiving, but this is rather a cliché and in practical terms can be frustrating and nonproductive. We have to feel there is some reciprocity. When I asked for the definition of a good friend in my questionnaire, here are some of the responses:

- A good friend is one who listens and doesn't judge.

- A good friend is someone who is genuinely pleased for you when you are successful and quietly supportive when you aren't.

- A good friend gives you their support even if they don't agree with what you've done.

- A good friend is someone who always has time for you.

Deciding to be a good friend isn't usually a conscious choice. But generally speaking we are now more inclined to pay attention to the nature of our friendships and make the effort to strengthen them than in the past. So assuming that there are people with whom we want to stay in touch, or get to know better, the following are important:

- Listen. Listen. Listen! Listen actively; respond to what you hear, ask questions.

- Be available. Don't turn down a visit or cut short a telephone call for some activity that can wait or be postponed. The friend has to come first.

- Avoid talking exclusively about yourself, your health, your children or the past. Truly no one is that interested, not even close friends.

- Make a serious effort to avoid negative comments. They sap other people's energy and that is now in short supply.

- Show appreciation and gratitude. Nobody is under any obligation to contact you, come and see you, do you a favour. If they do, count yourself lucky and make a point of saying how much you appreciate the effort. This is often neglected and we know from our own experience how we feel when we leave someone with the thought 'Well, I needn't have bothered'.

- Cultivate friendship by not letting it lapse. Emails, phone calls, letters or some form of contact show constructive interest and if you haven't heard from someone in a while, take the initiative to contact them.

- Offer hospitality (see below).

Hospitality

You have decided to take things more easily now, not to put yourself out unless you have to. You want to relax, not have to make a fuss about how you dress or what you do. This may lead you to think that having a friend or friends over to stay, for a meal or just a drink, can be effortless. Unfortunately that is exactly how it is perceived – that no effort was made. If you think back to those people whom you enjoyed visiting and those you didn't, you will realise that you enjoy visiting friends who:

- Greet you with a smile.

- Make some effort to welcome you.

- Have somewhere comfortable for you to sit.

- Offer you something to eat and drink.

- Ask you how you are.

- Listen to the reply.

- Don't grumble (too much) or talk about their aches and pains (exclusively).

- Don't make comments about your visits being too short or infrequent.

- Take into account your likes and dislikes, don't impose the quirks of their lifestyle on you.

- Thank you for having made the effort to visit them.

I make a big effort to see some of my friends, but when I get there, they don't even take the time to put a proper meal on the table.

Carol, 57

One of the things I loved about my aunt was that every visit was a celebration. She got in cakes and my favourite biscuits and even took the plastic covers off the settee! She was warm, welcoming and even though I knew she was sometimes tired or unwell, she never failed to make me feel important.

Gordon, 81

Bearing this in mind you should make a real effort to be welcoming; it is essential that you motivate people who visit you to come again by making sure their visit is comfortable, both physically and psychologically.

Letting 'friends' go

We all look through old address books or Christmas card lists and realise that we haven't seen some of the people behind the names for many, many years. While the odd letter or email can be comforting in that it makes us feel part of a wider social world as a reminder of happy and interesting times gone by, there are also all those contacts who no longer contribute anything to our lives and whom we feel are not worth our time and effort. We may decide to cross them off the list or, alternatively, choose to make a greater effort to renew and rekindle the friendship. We are often confronted with Roz's dilemma:

I find it very depressing to look through my address book. It isn't so much the friends who have died or gone away, it is more those that I am still in contact with but get no joy out of. I seem to be making a lot of effort for some of them with little in return and just wonder if that's the same for everyone at my age. I ask myself, should I still give the occasional call, is it worth it or should I just forget about them and concentrate on people whose company I really enjoy?

Roz, 69

Some people facing this choice will let these old, nostalgic contacts go, whereas others still actively search them out to renew and rekindle the friendship despite the gap in time and geography. The success of websites that bring friends together testifies to a need to renew old contacts – sometimes with heart-warming results. But often too much time has gone by and after a few initial meetings or emails, the relationship peters out. We have all moved on and there was always a reason why we didn't keep up with someone in the first place.

But it isn't only 'distance' friends we wonder about. Most of us go through a difficult time at one stage or another and it is in those tough times that we come to appreciate those friends who give us their support. We also learn, to our chagrin, that other friends don't, and to our surprise it isn't always our closest friends who are the most helpful.

I had a very dear friend for more than 30 years whom I was very fond of. But when I was diagnosed with cancer to my surprise she offered very little support. Although we talked on the phone she just insisted I would get better and that I shouldn't worry – not really the response I had hoped for. Since I've recovered I haven't really felt the same about her, I thought friendship was a about being there for someone when things are hard.

Martina, 82

It was quite distressing that dad's best friend didn't come to see him after his accident. My father kept on finding reasons why Charlie couldn't visit, but whatever the reason, he just didn't come. I was very disappointed for dad and after he died we didn't keep up with Charlie.

Trevor, 61

We can accept that some friends have a legitimate reason for not being able to help, they may have serious problems of their own or genuinely can't bear to see someone they love in trouble. But it is also true to say that not all friends are 'good friends' although this is a tough conclusion to reach.

Recognising those who are not good friends

Who are the friends who upset you most?

- Those who can't or won't put themselves out when you are distressed and offer little comfort.

- Those who rely on you to visit them.

- Those who are poor listeners.

- Those who don't share our values and with whom we no longer have anything in common.

- Those who are consistently negative or overbearing and leave us feeling drained or bulldozed.

- Those who communicate poorly on the pretext that they never use the telephone, email or the post.

I have a very small circle of friends and have known them all since I was quite young. But my friend Angie bothers me. I have always accepted her opinions and rather bossy manner, but my visits to her are now full of recriminations and after a while her comments get me down. I feel quite depressed and don't enjoy her company any more. What can I do? I get upset when I see her, but know that if I end the friendship it will leave a gap.

Melanie, 65

Melanie's choice is a truly difficult one. Would she feel better or worse if she let the friendship go? She's damned if she does and damned if she doesn't. Deep down is her fear of finding herself alone, a fear that is perfectly legitimate and which many of us share. Perhaps she already feels pretty isolated.

When we are younger we don't face this dilemma. If someone drops out of our social circle we have a fair chance that they can be replaced. Now, like Melanie, we can't be that sure that the gap will be filled, especially if we are losing someone who has accompanied us for a long period of our life.

Although a friend doesn't have to fill us with joy each time we see them, over a certain period of time there has to be some reward, however small. If we find ourselves with someone who offers neither moral nor practical support or if the communications from one year to the next are unrewarding, then we need to ask ourselves seriously, is this person worth our time and emotional investment?

Each of us will come to a different conclusion depending on what value we place on having a friend for old times' sake. We may enjoy any form of social contact, albeit an unsatisfactory one, for its own sake, or we may be confident that we can fill the gap – not necessarily with a replacement friend, which is unlikely if not impossible – but with some other more pleasurable activity.

Sandy had a similar experience to Melanie's:

Sandy's Story

I had a golfing partner a few years younger than me and over the years we were quite close. He would come to the house fairly often and we travelled together for championships. But he hardly ever asked us over to his place or out for meal. My wife pointed out that Jeff was a taker but I didn't see it that way. He was a bachelor and that was just his lifestyle. But then I began to get aches and pains and had to cut down a little on my golf, which annoyed Jeff. I could feel his frustration and his attitude toward me became more demanding. Finally with some hesitation I suggested he find another partner, but he didn't seem to want to do that. He just continued to make unpleasant remarks about me growing old. I finally had it out with Jeff who acted all hurt, but the time had come to say goodbye. I changed club and, amazingly, after all those years never saw him again. We talked maybe once or twice on the phone. It still hurts when I think about it and I do sometimes wonder what that friendship was all about, but to be frank, on a day-to-day basis, I am much better off now. I try to look back on the good times and feel lucky I had a close friend for the time that I did.

Sometimes we read that, like Sandy, we should weed out those friends who are unhelpful or who no longer contribute to our lives.

To increase our happiness we avoid people we've identified as egocentric and boring or critical and fearful. We seek out people who are interesting and optimistic. We must try to be around other people, especially happy people. [5]

But I think this is an approach that can be uncaring and uncharitable. We all know people who have problems and who rely on us much more for our support than we do on them. Most of us have one or two 'lame ducks' around us who sorely need our friendship. Not everyone in this world is pleasant, happy or good company, and if we get some satisfaction out of the relationship – if only because these friends give us their appreciation and make us feel better for having helped them – then that is reason enough to continue the friendship. Somehow it all balances out: some friends require more of us, whereas others give us a lot. We probably won't go out of our way to make friends in later life with people who are difficult but we shouldn't choose to abandon those we've known for a long time just because they take more than they give. Many of them give as much as they can.

Nevertheless if we know in advance that we don't enjoy someone's company or communications, then it is time to say 'no'. Most unsatisfactory contacts will die a natural death if we stop making an effort just for old times' sake.

Making new friends

This is really tough. I repeat, it is tough!

We are constantly being told to go out there and make new friends and younger friends at that. If we have specific interests and live in an area where there is a lot going on, then this is easier than if we live in a community that hasn't got much to offer or is more restrictive or isolated. Even if you are very flexible in your approach, are a 'joiner,' enjoy casual company and have few expectations, the chances that you will meet someone who has the time, energy and similarity of outlook enough to want to strike up a friendship with you are few and far between. Having a partner may make it easier to meet people initially but adds another, potentially complicating, dimension to the dynamic.

We do make friends later in life, often very good friends, but we are aware that they are precious and we are deeply grateful and appreciative.

Dan's Story

When his wife died, Dan sold their house in the country and moved to the town where he grew up as a boy. His childhood friends had all moved away and in fact he only had one contact, a cousin, still in the area. He threw himself into multiple activities, some of which he was genuinely interested in and some which he took up because he knew he would find company there. Five years on I asked Dan if he had made many friends. 'Oh, yes', he replied, 'lots'. Knowing the challenge it is to make friends I questioned him further. Dan then told me that, in fact, he rarely met up with anyone outside his organised activities and only twice had anyone invited him home. But that suited him fine; he certainly didn't miss closer contact and he had stopped being judgemental, taking what was on offer and appreciating it for what it was.

I don't think there is any magic formula for making friends at any age and certainly not when you are older; however, there are some evident truths that can form the basis of our choices:

- Take the first step; if you want to meet new people you will have to be proactive.

- Avoid being judgemental. You will need to be in contact with a lot of people before finding even one person with whom you feel at ease and who shares your outlook on life.

- Seek out a group or organised activity, even if this involves some travel or expense, because it is easier to get to know like-minded people if you share an interest with them.

- Join as many activities as you can afford or are available to you. You will whittle down what you do in the long term but the wider you cast your net, the greater your chances of meeting congenial people.

- Try to find an activity where people talk to each other. Not all activities, particularly classes, are interactive.

- Give priority to activities and people who are within easy reach.

- If there are no groups locally, or if you have physical, financial or social constraints, see if you could start a group in your own home.

- Join a chat-group on the Internet. It is not because this is a new form of friendship that it is any the less valid, many such groups meet up face-to-face at regular intervals.

- Be happy with whatever relationship does develop.

- Don't say 'no' to any invitation, people won't ask twice.

- Read the suggestion on page 116 (under Feeling lonely).

Most of us are trying to find a balance; strengthening bonds with friends we have already while remaining open to those new people we may be lucky enough to meet. If you feel the need to widen your social horizons you know it will take some effort and you will have to accept that the results may be disappointing. If you are content with the friends you have, you will make an effort to ensure that they remain with you for as long as possible. But the question of friendship is too important to be left to chance.

Chapter 15

Where we live

....

WE SEEM TO SPEND A LOT of time debating where to live, no doubt because we now have a real choice. A generation or two ago we stayed in our own homes until circumstances forced us into a care home or to live with our children. But today, as we stay more active for longer, we are faced with a multitude of possibilities that can be quite bewildering. Since our tastes, needs and circumstances are so varied it can be hard to know what advice to take and whose example to follow. We know too, that when we think about where to live the social, psychological, financial and physical aspects of this decision all overlap; while the head may be pulling one direction the heart may be pulling in another.

Anticipating the future

It is a question not only of where we live tomorrow but also of what happens when we look one step further ahead: when we may have more physical disabilities, need more medical care, easier access to support or can no longer drive. Life is unpredictable and we can't foresee every eventuality, but it still makes sense to determine what we want and then to plan for the more distant future as well as the immediate one.

You may be uncomfortable thinking about a time when your life will be different and prefer to let events take care of themselves. That choice, like any other, is yours to make, but having to make life-changing decisions, such as where to live, when you are under pressure or when you have been bereaved, are physically unwell or in financial difficulty, is not the same as making these decisions when you are still relatively independent and have the time and energy to rebound and adapt. We shouldn't live in middle age as though we were elderly but we would be wise to take old age into account. We have all known people who have found themselves in the distressing situation of having to make very important decisions about where to live under duress and most of us would want to avoid that for ourselves.

Staying where you are

A large number of us decide just to stay put. Our home is too full of memories, it still suits our needs and we cannot even entertain the idea of living anywhere else. We feel fairly confident that with just a few adjustments we can stay put until we need the sort of full-time care that can't be provided within our home. This choice is obviously the easiest, most comfortable option after the following have been considered:

- Can you afford the help you might need in the future to maintain your home and garden as you would wish in 10 years' time?

- Is that help available?

- If there is a change in your mobility, will you be able to modify your home? Get around without a car?

- Can your friends and family reach you easily if you can't get to them?

- Do you have access to the facilities you may need as the years go by?

- If you are not sure of the answers to the above, but your heart and head are playing at tug-of-war, are you prepared to make a move 10–15 years from now?

Sometimes, much as you would like to, staying where you are isn't a realistic possibility. Your home has become inappropriate for your changing needs. Sadly, or perhaps with relief, you conclude that you need to move to a place that needs less upkeep, will release some capital, save on running costs, or bring you nearer to sources of support.

You may choose to move to a different house in the same area. That way you retain your network of friends and services, while making your life easier by moving into housing which is more suited to an evolving lifestyle.

Prioritising needs

Any move involves considerable emotional and financial costs so it's only natural that it is a time of uncertainty and anxiety. But you can help yourself by prioritising your needs and thus simplifying your choice. Ask yourself these questions:

- What is it that makes a 'good home' for me personally?

- What contributes most to my mental and physical well-being? Family, friends, activities, climate, financial security, access to services, mobility, a beautiful home, garden, environment?

- What is my order of priority?

- Where can I compromise and what is non-negotiable? Is it really non-negotiable?

- How might these priorities change over the years?

- What will be the social, financial and practical results of making this move?

- Am I giving myself an escape route if I make a wrong decision?

These are classic questions and since you have probably been through moves before, it may just be more of the same despite the added pressure that this move may be the last one where you have real freedom of choice. It's different, however, if you decide to make a more drastic move involving either a complete change of lifestyle or living arrangements.

The dream, at home and abroad

We all have visions of a dream home. Now is probably the last opportunity we will have to fulfil that dream. Today more than ever before, the dream can involve a move abroad. At present we are seeing a huge exodus from the UK to favourable retirement areas, particularly within the European Union.

A drastic move to a different area and culture requires even more thought than moving within a familiar environment; and the more radical the change in lifestyle, the more you will need to be able to adapt and adjust to make the move a success. A new and challenging lifestyle can indeed be a dream come true but in no other circumstance is it quite so necessary to think through every implication of this choice. If you are thinking of moving abroad it is easy enough to find information concerning buying a property, tax, insurance, banking, exchange rates, inheritance laws, health care, year-round social activities and the weather. It's a little harder to find the answers to some other very pressing issues:

- Is my lifestyle shared with other people there? Have I identified those who share my values?

- How will I feel surrounded by people who do not share my outlook on life, my background?

- Where will I find my social and emotional support?

- How do I plan to see my family and old friends?

- How will their visits or my visits to them affect my budget?

- Can I envisage old age, reduced mobility and ill-health there? What picture comes to mind?

- What is the access to care? Can I find help in the home?

- What facilities are there for the elderly, how good are they and how much do they cost?

- If I know that staying in my new home in old age is not a realistic option, what financial provision am I making for an eventual further move later on? Or when my partner dies?

- Have I set aside or made provision for adequate capital if I need to move urgently?

A note of caution

So many people have successfully settled abroad and realised the dream of a lifetime that it seems a little churlish to strike a note of caution. However, it isn't all rosy. I live in an area where the British have settled in great numbers, usually in their fifties and sixties. Very few seem to have looked beyond the excitement of setting up a new home of their dreams. Regularly I hear of ill, bereaved or very elderly expats who have had to return 'home' to the UK in stressful circumstances either because they don't have the financial means to get back into the housing market, or because they left it too late to make that choice with serenity and proper planning.

Throughout Europe this previous generation of expats, now in their eighties or older, should serve as a warning. They are finding the going tough as they realise that although excellent medical help may be on hand, assisted care is another matter. The care infrastructure in continental European countries is often expensive, unfamiliar, inappropriate or non-existent. It remains to be seen whether over the next ten to 20 years, there will be adequate development of care structures, in whatever form, to cater for our generation. At present, Age Concern in Spain for instance says they get 12,000 calls a year from Britons who cannot find the care they need.[6]

But even moving to another part of the UK can be a challenge:

> I dreamt of being here all my life, and when I inherited some money decided to go for it. What can I say? After the fun of doing the place up and exploring the area, I now find myself in a world of unfamiliar people. I'm disappointed. Mind you I just couldn't have known, I did do all the homework before moving, but didn't think enough about what I would be doing after the initial excitement was over.
>
> Matty, 57

It wasn't possible for Matty to foresee every eventuality and, as she says, she did read up about all the practical issues before making the move. Saying goodbye to a dream is extremely hard, but the choice she faces now is whether to stay or to go. If she chooses to go, the quicker the better, but that supposes she has another, better, place to go to and the resources to move. What Matty found to her cost, is that there is more to moving than changing home.

Moving in with a friend or the family: the ripple effect

> I live in a granny flat and I'm so happy here. I do sometimes wonder if my son is as pleased with the arrangement as I am, but I feel they are.
>
> Hanna, 76

For Hanna this has been the ideal solution where everyone is happy, and there are many success stories such as hers. There are also many which do not have such a happy ending.

> A year ago my daughter married and together with her husband decided to run a small hotel. They asked me to join them and I sold my house, invested a little capital with them and moved into an annex of the hotel. But after only 6 months I knew the arrangement couldn't work out long term. I have decided to make a clean break now and recoup my losses. So I am moving yet again and hope that at 67 I can begin a new life. But some good things have come out of this; I am proud that I can still make independent decisions, and a quick decision in this case was essential.
>
> June, 67

June was very lucky, she was able to withdraw her money from her daughter's business, and was well enough to make a second move quite soon after the first. She had an optimistic view of life, which enabled her to act decisively and envisage a positive outcome.

Although moving in with a close friend or family may be a wonderful solution for some of us, on the whole you should be wary of sharing your home. Even when housing is adjacent to or independent of the main accommodation you soon realise that everyday contact is not at all the same as the occasional visit. There is a ripple effect; the new relationship changes the dynamics not just between the principals involved but between each and every member of the extended household and beyond, into their social networks. Sometimes other family members are relieved that someone is keeping an eye on you, or they may feel aggrieved that you have opted to live with one person rather than another or with someone they don't particularly like. Your feelings are more important than theirs but there can be widespread repercussions that you would do well to consider.

> Our mother had a very close friend, some 20 years younger than her and Mother became very dependent on her until finally she suggested that Fay should come to live with her. We never liked Fay much and when she was running Mum's house things went from bad to worse. We are sure that she sponged off my mother and took some of her personal possessions but Mum just didn't want to hear what we were telling her. When Mum died we made sure that Fay left the house at once and took nothing with her.
>
> Sue, 77

Understanding possible problems

Fay, in the situation described above, would probably have a very different story to tell and this illustrates just how sensitive the issue of family living arrangements can be. Before you make choices about sharing your home, consider the following:

- Make sure that all the issues have been fully discussed with everyone involved, not just your direct relative or friend.

- If at all possible, give the new arrangement a trial period.

- Ask yourself why you have been invited to make this arrangement? Is it out of duty, financial concern, friendship; in other words: what is their motivation?

- Consider how much independence you will have, both now and in the future.

- Work out what your financial contribution will be. How will any financial changes affect inheritance issues?

- Think how you will maintain your privacy as well as theirs.

- Think what will happen when you are no longer mobile, or unable to use your own car.

- How much do you expect to be included in their social life? Is this a mutual expectation? How do you all feel about it?

- How will you feel if they go on holiday, have a party, go out without you? (be honest here!)

- How will you spend your holidays?

- How well do you get on, not just with your direct family or friend but with their social circle and their extended family? (If there is the slightest tension before the move, it will be multiplied a hundredfold once you are in close proximity.)

- Are you prepared to move into a different form of housing if/when you need more care, or are you hoping they will still look after you?

- What safety valve do you have? Do you have somewhere, a friend's house maybe, where you can escape if things get tense?

- What will it mean for other friends and family, and how will they react if you make this arrangement? How will you deal with this?

- What will happen to you if for any reason your friend or family has to move from the area or change house?

My mother gave my sister a large sum to enable her to buy a house big enough to include a couple of rooms to house her. After four years my sister suddenly sold the house and moved away leaving my mother to go into residential care. I don't know who is more upset and angry, me or my mother.

Ava, 60

I have come to live with my son on his farm and the house is very comfortable and I am well looked after. But it was a mistake because my social life revolves around theirs. I can't drive any longer and I miss the shopping and my friends. Unfortunately I don't have the money any more or the energy to move out and I wish I had given more thought to my later years when I still had more options open to me.

Bertha, 84

If you have any misgivings before you set up home with someone else, don't! If you tell yourself, 'But I don't have any other choice', you are mistaken. There are always other options. It is unwise to share a household unless everyone concerned realises exactly what is involved and accepts that great adjustments will have to be made.

Looking beyond yourself

While giving full priority to your own needs you shouldn't forget the wider ramifications of moving. If you change locality as well as housing you are not just making a geographical move, you are making a huge social change as well. Your entire social network will be modified. It will be as though you have shaken up a kaleidoscope; none of the pieces will ever fall in quite the same place again. So you need to be prepared not just to change the furniture around but to change your social relationships as well.

When choosing a new home, you should give due weight to those who make up your social world, many of whom are also growing older, to how accessible you are to friends and family (or even new acquaintances) who might like to drop in.

We lived in a lovely Victorian house and we really wanted to stay put but the front steps became a serious issue for our elderly parents and several of our friends. We have moved to a flat, more for them than ourselves, although we can see that it will make sense for us too in the future.

Adele, 60

I have moved into a wonderful flat in a sheltered housing development. The atmosphere is really friendly and everyone is very supportive. My only regret is that there isn't a spare room and I have to book and pay for a guest room several floors below mine. I can see that friends are reluctant to stay because they know it costs me money and since we are out in the country, nobody can just drop in as they used to do when we lived in town. The choice has been a very hard one but the advantages far outweigh the disadvantages and I feel safe, secure and among people I have a lot in common with.

Gordon, in his seventies

If you downsize, remember the social implications of space – or lack of it. If you want people to come and stay, have an extra bedroom; if you're used to a garden, find a place with room for some plants; if you enjoy entertaining, have adequate space to do this. This is quite apart from having a place to put a bicycle, wheelchair or tools.

My home is now so full of furniture I don't even have the space to do a jigsaw puzzle, play with the grandchildren or put up my sewing machine.

Polly, 73

This is Polly's choice; we all know homes that are crammed full of furniture to the detriment of adequate living space. But if you want family and friends to come to see you, you need to provide them with a comfortable place to sit, eat, be entertained and even sleep.

Choosing where to live is obviously a life-changing decision and in later years we are very aware that there isn't as much room to manoeuvre as before. Yes, we still have time to correct a mistake as June did (described on page 206), but we would prefer to get it right first time around. But none of us is gifted with a crystal ball, and if we make a mistake it is vital to admit the error quickly and choose again.

The one thing we can be absolutely sure of is that by the time we are in our eighties, we will find ourselves in changed circumstances. Few of us will enjoy the same lifestyle at 85 as we did at 70 or 55, so we need to think beyond the next few years and act accordingly. Indeed, a move on retirement may not be the last we make but it is important that this move should not jeopardise the next. Be aware that circumstances may change dramatically, and build future change into the equation.

Part 4

Our Money

Introduction

··

THIS PART IS NOT ABOUT how to manage your income, there are many books on retirement devoted solely or largely to money questions. Instead, it looks at the social and emotional issues that influence your financial decisions, because when you make choices involving money you are no more rational than when, say, choosing a partner. In the long term you will be more comfortable with any financial decision you make if you take into account the return on your emotional investment as well as interest rates!

How much money you actually have and the income-generating aspects of your finances are important. But so, too, are your subjective feelings about how rich or poor you are. Your perceptions and reality may be two quite different things and now may well be the time to take a look at some long-standing beliefs and habits.

The following chapters concentrate on what you choose to spend your money on and on whom. They are based on the assumption that although most of us are on a more or less fixed and, sometimes, reduced income you do have some room for manoeuvre, however small. This is not to ignore the fact that a huge number of pensioners fall below the poverty line, and it would be presumptuous to think that there is much meaningful choice when any money you have barely covers the cost of food and heat.

Thinking about money

When it comes to managing our money, by the time we are in or near our sixties we've done it for long enough to feel that we know what works for us. However, we realise that there are times when a professional opinion can make all the difference and so many of us will consider taking advice about how to manage our income, our investments or the sudden windfall that we may be lucky enough to receive. We may well need help to draw together the threads of various pension and savings schemes to make the most of what we have during retirement.

At the same time we are all too aware that financial advice can be completely contradictory: 'At all costs, avoid making a home-equity loan' versus 'The money you can raise on your home will be the greatest source of financial security in your later years.' And that's to say nothing of the endless television ads and direct-mail circulars we're bombarded with, encouraging us to take out one insurance policy after the next to 'give us peace of mind in our old age'. It takes a clear head to steer a course through the minefield of sales pitches. But on these issues there is plenty of help out there.

However, when it comes to deciding how to spend money rather than invest it, advice is thin on the ground. Frequently we find ourselves making choices in a vacuum because we feel uneasy about discussing emotional or moral issues connected with money either with a paid advisor, friends or family. We are unaware that people of our age face similar dilemmas and have to make the same difficult choices as ourselves.

The specifics of our generation

We are, for the most part, better off than our parents' generation but we also have greater long-term financial requirements. Ours is the first generation that can expect to live actively into our eighties (and even beyond) and needs to plan financially for a period of 20 years or longer. As such, we have no role models or reliable financial blueprints by which to measure whether or not we are making the right decisions. And by the time we have learned through experience, it may be too late, as sadly all too many of us have learned recently to our cost with failed pension fund and investment schemes. Many of us have seen the grief caused to parents forced to sell their home to pay for long term nursing care and realise that without adequate provision this is a likely outcome for us too.

Since Yuppies and Dinkies, a new category has popped up, the 'SKIs' (Spending the Kids' Inheritance), which assumes that there's a trend for those beyond 55 to spend their money before they die, based on some new found hedonism. In fact, instead of throwing our money at non-stop Caribbean cruises, we are far more likely to spend it on supplementing pensions, helping out children, partners and friends who are facing financial pressures, as well as keeping up interests and activities over an extended period beyond retirement.[1]

If you are already retired you will probably be living at

the financial level which you had anticipated. Unlike younger generations we paid into schemes that are relatively reliable and generous, and although many of us have to adjust to less spending power, we still hope to have enough money for some leisure, travel and other activities well into extreme old age. This is very different from those now in their forties who do not have the security of such guaranteed pension schemes.

We may accept the idea that money doesn't necessarily make us happy, and, as we grow older appreciate that health and time are more precious than financial wealth. Nevertheless, feeling that we have 'enough' money, whatever amount that may be for each of us individually, underpins almost every other aspect of our lives playing an essential role in how comfortable and secure, and therefore, how 'happy' we feel.

> My need to feel secure seems to have increased with age and for me security means enough money. Not masses, but enough.
>
> Hassan, 57

> I think my concerns regarding money in later life aren't so much about today but about whether or not what I have will be adequate in the future. To spend now or to save for the end of my life, that is the question!
>
> Isabella, 66

Sometimes, however, we read that satisfaction in later life is not at all about money but about joy and inner peace. As I discussed in Chapter 9 (Spiritual life) this may be true to some degree but the idea that we don't need much money in later life underestimates the contribution that money makes to feelings of security and the satisfaction we get, like everyone else, with the purchase of goods and services. It assumes that as we age, we live detached from the rest of the world, on some other plane, divorced from commercial realities. This not only belittles us and our financial concerns, it also undervalues our economic status and spending power.

What I discuss here are the issues that were raised most often with me and are not always adequately addressed in the press or media. I have grouped some of the spending choices we face under the Chapter headings 'Money and You' (discussing our subjective view of money) and 'Money and Others' (covering the financial expectations that others have of us).

Chapter 16

Money and you

··

W E ALL CARRY ATTITUDES about money that affect how we decide to spend it. Understandably, our feelings about money can help us when we are trying to decide whether we want to buy something that would make life easier for us and that we may not have had the chance of buying before.

How much is enough?

The answer to the question 'How much money is enough?' is entirely personal. A spendthrift never has enough, but then neither has the keenest saver. As we grow older our spending patterns and how we think of money may be modified, but are unlikely to change fundamentally. If you've been prudent or profligate all your life, you'll continue to be so in retirement; but equally, if your life has been plagued by poor financial decisions or inadequate income, this might be an opportunity to take a new look at how you view money and how you make decisions about spending it.

Everyone seems to agree that it is frustrating talking to friends and family about money since everyone has different ideas about necessity and luxury. 'Saving', 'economy', 'indulgence' and 'waste' are all relative terms. The amount of money each of us needs in order to feel financially secure and in control of our lives varies enormously from person to person and has little to do with the actual sums in our bank account. Very often, decisions that appear to be about money are more to do with perceptions of what's worth spending money on.

> David really can't manage the garden as well as before. I'm desperate to get some help in but he says we can't afford it and he can still do it even though it is obvious the garden is becoming neglected.
>
> Babs, 54

> When I was a boy, taking a taxi was unthinkable; I still feel guilty when I have to take a cab somewhere.
>
> Nathan, 59

I'm sure this sounds familiar. But why do we so often have a problem spending money while those who are younger don't?

Evolving attitudes and values

How we spend and save has been conditioned not only by our upbringing but also by a specific set of values arising from the war and post-war years. Financially most of us have been extremely lucky to live through a period where the state was still able to provide a generous safety net of services, and most of us have adequate pensions. Psychologically however, we are not quite so fortunate.

We are torn between the thrift of our parents whose spending habits were conditioned naturally by the war years, and which we find irritatingly penny-pinching (turning off the lights when leaving a room even briefly), and the instant gratification and aspirational spending habits of younger generations, which many of us consider extravagant and short-sighted. We may be willing to spend money on our home and garden but find it almost impossible to buy ourselves a bottle of special whisky or a bunch of flowers for no other reason than because we want to. We know we don't need to acquire more material goods yet we hesitate to participate in the growing trend towards purchasing services, even when they might transform our lives.

Younger people don't seem to have a problem with this; they don't think twice about taking a taxi, eating out or buying prepared foods or paying to have a loose button sewn on. Yet through a lifelong habit of economy and inherited values, pleasing ourselves is often not part of our mental make up. Although we pay lip service to the idea that as we grow older our time, energy and good health, both physical and mental, are more precious than money, most of us are still reluctant to pay for something if there is 'nothing to show for it'.

Bringing ourselves to spend what we have

Most of us have neither too little nor too much; our income is adequate – whatever that means to each of us personally – and although we don't much welcome suggestions from others as to how we 'should' be spending our income, it does make good sense to take on board that our money should contribute to the enrichment of our mental and physical environments. We have to marshal our resources and find pleasure wherever we can; it's now or never. And to do this most of us need to overcome our reluctance to spend money on 'non-essentials', to stop feeling that buying services or 'treating' ourselves is somehow sinful or an unnecessary luxury.

If you find it hard to spend money on yourself, here are some suggestions that may help:

- Overcome the idea that certain goods or services are unnecessary or 'not for people like me'. When you find yourself saying 'it's ridiculous to spend that amount of money on …' you should remember that if a product or service is on the market, other people are buying it despite the price. Why them and not you? The people who are buying those goods and services are probably no richer than you but have chosen that particular pleasure or the convenience that their money can provide.

- Learn to accept that the money you have is there in order to make your *present* life easier. To make savings now through fear of penury in extreme old age is to do your future self an injustice. Life may be very long, yes, but may also be very short and you need to enjoy it while you can. Now is the time to treat yourself well because there may not be a more appropriate time in the future. Infirmity or plain world-weariness will prevent you spending quite so happily later on. The recent Lufthansa advertisement put it brilliantly: 'If you don't fly first class, your children will.' Yes, the money you have earned and saved can be spent on yourself now, rather than on someone's inheritance later on.

I went out to replace some broken cups and suddenly saw this wonderful bone china dinner service. I had never had any proper china and this was exactly what I had always dreamed of. I thought 'why not?' and I just went ahead and bought it even though it was an absolute extravagance. I decided to use it all the time and although my friends say I am quite mad, I feel good whenever I lay the table. Buying that service was quite out of character, but I enjoy it each and every day.

Rachel, 73

- You can begin with small things and continue from there. Buy yourself a beautiful house-plant, call your friend in Australia, take the car to the car wash. Note the pleasure, or relief, it gives you; see how little in fact it affects your overall budget and let this be the start of an on-going habit.

- Get in as much household help as you need or can afford. Most of us can afford some help, and the physical and psychological relief when someone shares the work is certainly worth the cost. If buying in help can help maintain or improve your lifestyle, so much the better.

- Pay extra for increased comfort. For example, upgrade travel arrangements as much as finances allow. Pay the 10 per cent more for a better hotel room – the memory of the ocean view will be with you long after you have forgotten the cost.

- Take a taxi or minicab when you are tired or in a hurry. It really isn't an extravagance, it's a convenience that helps to conserve your increasingly limited reserves of energy.

- Pay what it costs to give yourself small, everyday pleasures. The extra options in the new car, the out-of-season fruit, the more luxurious toiletries.

- Make good use of the convenience foods and services on offer, such as home delivery or prepared vegetables. Do you really feel better for having cleaned the potatoes yourself?

Living on less

Many of us find ourselves with a lower income in later life, and on the whole we will have foreseen this and made appropriate adjustments or arrangements. But some of you may be victims of failing pension funds or the vagaries of the stock market, or just find that your financial reality is harder to deal with than you thought.

Money and status in western society are closely linked, and while few of you talked to me about cash and investments, I heard a lot of discussion about loss of social standing. It is one of the tougher issues many of us face, but not one that always gets a proper hearing.

We both had the prospect of comfortable pensions but Andrew made some serious investment mistakes and we are now on a much reduced income. We have kept on our large high-maintenance house and to those outside the family it looks as though we live much as before. But I haven't bought any new clothes for several years, we can't afford to go on holiday and have to make constant economies, even paying for a car park is sometimes a problem. We have a good circle of friends but they all have far more money than we do now and

we find it hard to keep up; Andrew won't even consider selling the house but I truly wonder if we have made the right
choice.

Michelle, 63

Michelle is not going to get much sympathy from those who
feel that her problem is one for the privileged, but, in fact,
the choice is the same for everyone, whatever your level of
income. Is it better to make one big saving in order to avoid
radical change (downsizing your home, forgoing holidays,
giving up the second car)? Or, you could make small, day-
to-day economies such as buying cheaper food, cutting out
cinema or pub visits, or, like Michelle, buying fewer clothes.
Whatever the sums of money involved and whatever others
say, this is a very personal choice, since what is vital to us
may be quite irrelevant to someone else.

If you get depressed at the thought of not being able to
afford a weekend break, the occasional restaurant meal or
giving something to friends and family, you may find it
easier to take one big step to change your circumstances,
such as selling the family home. Then you can continue to
live comfortably afterwards, rather than endure the ongoing
stress of small economies.

But if your social standing depends on our home, garden
and material lifestyle, any amount of sacrifice feels worthwhile in order to keep this up. Those who struggle to maintain a way of life that seems to others to have little relevance
as the years go by, come in for a lot of criticism. But if feelings of self-worth are intimately bound up with a certain
lifestyle, you will be seriously distressed about changing this
in later life. Selling a home or resigning from an expensive
club may make financial sense but be socially quite unacceptable.

Except for the lucky few, we have all had to reconsider expenses that once we took in our stride: club membership fees, magazine subscriptions, restaurant meals or regular theatre visits. And if we do have to make economies it helps enormously if others in our social circle are cutting back at the same time. Any unease or distress we may experience is hopefully counterbalanced by an altered approach to material things and by new benefits that later life can bring.

Using money differently

When you need to make decisions about using your money differently, the following questions may help in setting priorities:

- Is the choice facing me really about money or is it about lifestyle?

- On the income I now have, what kind of a lifestyle can I realistically afford? How acceptable is this to me?

- If I continue living as I did before, will I begin to resent the cost? Will the expense be uppermost in my mind and spoil the pleasure that I once had?

- How important is it to me socially to maintain my former lifestyle, and for how long can I keep it up?

- If I give something up, what else might I gain, in the short term, in the long term?

- Have I considered alternative options? (Sharing magazine subscriptions, exchanging homes, and so on.)

- Have I thought through the indirect consequences of making this choice? (For example, moving to a smaller home may mean that it is harder for friends and family to stay.)

- Am I upset by reducing this particular expense, or is it the feeling that this is the beginning of a general slide into an even more reduced lifestyle?

Having too much

Not having enough money is a fairly common concern. But having too much also causes difficulties and, personally, I was surprised how often this issue was mentioned, usually in the context of keeping and maintaining friendships.

While some of our friends or family members may have considerably more – or considerably less – money than we do, generally speaking we are socially most comfortable with those who have a similar income and standard of living. We naturally tend to gravitate towards people who share our values and lifestyle, and both of these are shaped to a large extent by money, so it is unrealistic to think that income and friendship aren't linked. We may not spend our money in exactly the same way as our friends but, generally, we socialise without different incomes or spending patterns becoming an issue.

Changing values

People often change their behaviour when their financial circumstances change, and with a decrease or increase in wealth comes a shift in their values, however subtle. When we were younger we saw our own and our friends' fortunes change gradually over time and either we still had enough in common to link us over the years or we have drifted apart. Now, however, people we know can suddenly become wealthier through an investment windfall, a generous company handshake or an inheritance. The impact is more immediate and any potential change in lifestyle is more noticeable.

> I live in a small community where we all have a similar income and lifestyle. But a year ago I came into a very generous inheritance and although everyone knows I received some money, they don't realise quite how much. I am now able to afford all sorts of things I couldn't before and no longer need to be as cautious as most of my friends. I don't know whether just to spend as freely as I would like, or even help some of my friends out, or pretend I have the same income as before. On the one hand I'm frightened of losing my friends but on the other it doesn't seem to make much sense to have the money and not use it.
>
> George, 70

> My close friend Carol married a little while ago for the third time and I was really pleased for her. Anthony, the man she married, is very nice and we get on well. It seems silly to say that his money is the problem but it is. He is immensely wealthy and somehow makes me feel inadequate although I'm not badly off myself. Over the last couple of years Carol and I have just grown apart. They are really very generous but I can't reciprocate in a way which suits Anthony and I just feel disconnected from their lifestyle. Carol is still very friendly and I feel guilty that I don't feel the same way any more about our friendship. I have mentioned my feelings to her, but her reaction is that friendship has nothing to do with money.
>
> Rivka, 62

So what happens when you suddenly have more money than those around you, when you no longer have shared financial concerns and are able to afford extras, holidays, home help or consumer goods that your friends consider luxuries – or perhaps have never considered at all? You can find yourself in a potentially awkward and embarrassing situation. I think you have the following choices:

- To acknowledge that you have more money.

- To pretend that the financial situation hasn't changed.

- To find a middle way.

Acknowledging you have more money

You may be inclined to tell everyone how lucky you are to have become richer later in life. If so, you need to be aware that for every person who will be genuinely pleased for you there will be others who will feel envious or inadequate and, like Rivka, feel that they can no longer relate to you as they did before. Offering to pick up the expensive restaurant bill or pay for a holiday weekend, or even bringing a generous gift, lovely as this is, may only deepen the divide.

You may say, 'Well that's their problem. I'm being generous, why can't they accept it graciously?' But you have to recognise that the connection between money and status is so strong that to your friends, if not to yourself, you may now be in a different 'class' from them, with the associated discomfort this can cause.

Pretending nothing has changed

On the other hand, participating in discussions on how to get the best deal on the garden furniture or save money by doing your own plumbing, knowing that neither of these issues really matters to you, is ultimately frustrating. While going through the charade means you might remain 'acceptable' to your group of friends, it keeps you at a psychological distance and always having to play a role.

The middle way

If you want to keep up with former friends and family, adopting a middle way can work even though it requires some thought, and you may feel it reduces some of the spontaneity which underpins the joy of long-standing relationships.

Here are some suggestions:

- Do not pretend that you have less money than you really have.

- However, be cautious and circumspect. Do not talk about money except to your very closest friends and even then be diplomatic.

- When appropriate, tell your friends that you are happy to share your good fortune with them and make them part of the new experience, but avoid being condescending or belittling what, for others, are large sums of money.

- Renew your efforts not to let your change in circumstances influence the values and attitudes that bind your social circle together.

- In your social life, let others around you make decisions involving money. Let them pick out the theatre seats, the restaurant, and so on, and even if you prefer something better, never say so.

- When you're out with friends, pay your share but no more. If an outing is 'your treat', don't flaunt your money; choose somewhere that you know your friends will like, and never reveal what it costs.

- If you're making arrangements to go out with friends, always consult them about their preferred price range of tickets or venues.

- If you want to buy an expensive car or go on a luxury holiday, just go ahead and do so. If people make a comment, let it pass or just say, 'Yes, I'm lucky that at present I can afford that.' Don't say, 'Yes, I got a cheap deal.' No one is fooled.

- Be discreet in your spending. You don't have to show photos of the luxury Caribbean holiday or talk about prices. Others will guess what things cost but that is not the same as hearing it from you outright.

- If you want to buy expensive clothes or cars or perhaps restyle your home, do so in the knowledge that your lifestyle may be admired but may also give rise to gossip and negative comment. You can't win, but do try to have a sense of humour about it.

- Be explicit in your appreciation of friendship when invited. Some people will apologise for the simplicity of their meal/home/welcome. Make it clear that their friendship is always more important than the surroundings.

- Avoid situations where the money gap is obvious, such as shopping sprees, holidays and evenings out on the town, unless you've already established what's acceptable to everyone, and stick with this.

Ever since I was a lad, me and a group of mates have been supporters of our local football club and go to matches all over the world. I've done very well in life but they're all still in my hometown and live pretty modestly; they often find it hard to get the fares together. Whenever we have to travel I join them at the hotel. They have no idea I travel business class, exactly how I earn my living or where I live. Although I sometimes feel a bit of a cheat, these people are important to me and the pretence is the price I pay for their friendship.

John, 60

Chapter 17

Money and others

··

B ALANCING OUR INCOME AND expenditure would be relatively simple if we only had to take ourselves into
account. But we're not alone – others have financial expectations of us too. Many of us share our money with a partner, and we also have financial commitments involving
elderly parents, friends or adult children that are not always
predictable or within our control.

What we do with our money is heavily influenced by our
social environment and how others, including a partner,
think we should be spending our money. Questions about
our lifestyle and the expectations others have of us (or
which we believe they have) may now, when our earning
capacity is usually curtailed, come into sharp focus. As we
will see from the typical cases below, many of us face a
financial choice that not only involves income but also
social, emotional and psychological issues as well.

Money and children

Most of us were brought up to be financially independent at an early age. The situation today is quite different and we often find ourselves unprepared financially or emotionally to deal with the needs, demands and expectations of those younger than us.

> My daughter, now in her early thirties, is struggling to make it as a professional photographer. She is convinced that success is just around the corner but in the meantime we help her out every month with the rent. I don't know if we should be doing this.
>
> Cecilia, 65

At what point do we tell our children that they have to be financially independent? How often have we heard friends say that their teenage children will have to learn to stand on their own two feet when they leave home (or at some arbitrarily chosen age), only to find that parental ties were too strong and that the children in fact continue to receive financial support or live at home long after the supposed cut-off date?

Almost all of us, who were able to do so, have at one time or another given money to our children against our better judgement, or know someone who has. Surprisingly often it is one parent who secretly gives the kids extra money. And increasingly, as they struggle to get on the housing ladder or find a job, we help out our children with quite considerable amounts.

The rational view is that children need to learn financial independence. After all, we did! People tell us, 'Don't feel guilty, it's your money', 'They have to learn to fend for themselves', 'At your time of life, why do you think you have to help them so much?' The reality is that when we see our children in difficulty (and yes, 'difficulty' is a relative term), we instinctively want to help them no matter how 'grown up' they are or what others say we should or shouldn't do. The emotional factor is every bit as important, if not more important, than the rational.

Making the choice to help

Deciding to help our children financially is not always a comfortable choice. Our instincts tell us one thing, our bank statements another, and we may receive little thanks or reward for putting ourselves out. So what are your options and on what basis can you make a decision?

Here are some questions to ask yourself:

- Can I really afford to help financially, or am I doing so at some cost to my own comfort, knowing that at this stage in my life it is unlikely that I can regain the sum I am paying out?

- Is my child in real financial difficulty or am I helping to maintain a lifestyle which I don't think is necessary (although the recipient might!) – are they going off on long holidays, buying designer clothes, and so on?

- Is the child making any effort themselves to increase their income, such as getting a job, seeking promotion, look for other financial solutions?

- Do I feel that if I refuse financial support the child will love me less, or no longer come to see me? Will this choice change our relationship, maybe for the worse?

- Does this situation bring me some satisfaction or does it make me angry and upset? Do I feel appreciated or exploited?

After asking yourself these questions you may conclude *either* that on balance the effort is worth it, *or* that you really can't continue handing out subsidies, although you may dread having to broach the subject.

- If the latter is the case, why not try this step-by-step approach?

- Firstly, remember that many parents go through this. You're not the exception and you're not 'wrong' to feel the way you do.

- Decide in your own mind exactly why you have chosen to stop the money (for example, your own financial difficulties, your perception that they should now be more independent). And stick to your decision.

Being firm

The following ideas may help you to remain firm in making your decisions:

- Mentally go over all the arguments that you expect to hear as your child expresses surprise and hurt that you're 'doing this to them'. Prepare your counter-arguments.

- State clearly why the situation has changed, and do not be persuaded in the course of the discussion to backtrack.

- If you feel the pressure is too great, make no commitment in the heat of the moment but tell them that you will think about it.

- If you decide to help out financially but want it to be understood that there is a cost to you, say you are happy to continue to give financial support but that from now on the money will be a loan and not a gift (knowing that family loans are rarely repaid).

- Alternatively, say that you will continue financial support but only for the next six (or however many) months.

- Or say that you will give them love and support in any other way they want, but no longer any money. For example, they can join you in your holiday home this summer, use the car to go to the job interview, and so on.

- You will still give them the occasional sum for a specific expense, for example a training course, a new suit for an interview, etc.

Money and relatives

With the rise in the number of partnerships and recomposed families, increasingly we find ourselves supporting family members with whom we or our partners do not have a strong relationship. What was taken for granted in a traditional family may now present us with a financial dilemma.

> My partner and I have always seen eye to eye on money matters but I now find myself having to pay large sums for my mother's care home. My partner has been willing, so far, to contribute more than his share to our joint expenses so that we can still maintain our former lifestyle but I sense growing resentment about this on his part and I feel guilty and under pressure to choose between my mother and my partner.
>
> Shaun, 59

Let's look at what the right side of the brain is telling you: that as a couple you are committed to sharing the good and the bad; it just so happens that it is your elderly relative and not your partner's who needs expensive care. You would, you believe, do the same for him/her.

The left side however, is saying that this situation is unfair on your partner, wasn't foreseen when you set up a household together and what was a balanced relationship is now out of kilter. You feel guilty and torn between your responsibility towards your family member and commitment to your partner.

In this case it really helps to separate the emotional issues from the financial, since discussions – and disputes – about money often camouflage deeper issues. If the emotional issues are resolved, the problems around money can often be resolved too.

The emotional issues

The following questions will help you look at the emotional issues involved:

- Is this guilt you feel over the unfair expense of caring for your elderly relative self-imposed or has your partner actually done or said something to confirm this view?

- Have you discussed this openly or is it an ongoing but unspoken issue?

- What is it exactly that is making your partner resentful? Is it the money, or perhaps the time you are spending on caring for someone else?

- What would each of you do if the situation were reversed?

- If there is real financial stress, what can you do to prevent it disrupting your relationship?

- Have your feelings of guilt made you behave differently towards your partner? Are you being more aggressive perhaps or less open?

- Is your partner using the situation to exert control or emotional blackmail?

- Have you (and other members of your family) expressed adequate thanks and appreciation to your partner for his or her support?

- Do the terms of your partnership need to be re-examined?

The financial issues

The following questions might help you think about the financial issues involved:

- Have you really considered all the available financial options open to your relative? Or have you decided to take on this financial responsibility without due consideration of the alternatives, or perhaps for some other reason?

- If you conclude that you must pay for, or contribute to, your relative's care does your partner agree with your conclusions?

- If your partner thinks that your relative could be in a less expensive home, that other family members should contribute more, or that you should use other resources available, have you considered that she or he may be right?

- Have you been able to state clearly to him or her why you don't agree?

- If there will be inherited money, can your partner be repaid at a later date?

- Is there some way you can compensate for your partner's extra financial burden, by taking on more household responsibilities, or reducing some of your own expenses?

- If your partner agrees to carry more of the cost of caring for your relative, is the rest of your family aware of this?

- What are the financial implications for both of you of this increased cost, and how can you factor this in to your own plans for the future?

Who needs the money more?

Ideally, within a family, everyone agrees that money should go where it is most needed. In reality that is not always the case. Money plays a symbolic as well as a financial role and the sharing out of money is often perceived as the sharing out of parental love. While this is painfully familiar to many of us – as parents and as children – it isn't rational. For every child, no matter how adult, what parents decide to do with their money and possessions is highly charged. The emotional issues are inextricable from the practical and so our feelings *do* influence our decisions about who will get what and how much. Bearing in mind that it is impossible to eliminate emotion from any decision, the best we can do is to see how we can be fair while ensuring that our money goes where it's most needed. The most common scenario is this:

I have several children and one of them, through no fault of his
own, now needs more financial help than the others; but how
can I help him out without upsetting the rest of the family?

James, 79

Is the permanently hard-up son with several children more
worthy of parental support than the daughter who would
like to set up her own business? Should money be given to
a family friend who is finding it hard to make ends meet? Or
to bail out a sister who has landed herself in debt? Is there a
hierarchy of need? If there is plenty of money around these
choices are easier but for most of us the situation is one of
either/or, so here are some points to consider before making
your choice:

- There is great satisfaction to be had from seeing the
  pleasure and thanks that a gift of money or possessions
  can bring. Gifts in our lifetime are worth twice as much
  as after our death.

- However, to avoid resentment, any money given has to
  be given unconditionally. All too often 'gifts' to our nearest and dearest come with strings attached – exhortations
  to spend the money wisely, or in a specific way. For the
  recipient, it makes the gift a burden with the result that it
  cancels out the pleasure and thanks that you hoped to
  have when you made the gift in the first place.

- When you choose to help out a friend or family member
  there will almost certainly be a ripple effect through the
  rest of the family or close social circle.

- To avoid repercussions from the rest of the family you
  may decide to loan the money. But we know statistically
  that family loans are rarely repaid. The family may be

aware of this and want to be sure this isn't a gift in disguise. Decide what the terms of the loan are and make them known to all concerned.

- You can give the money and not inform the rest of the family. This can seem like the best option at the time, but, if at some later stage, the truth comes out it can be very destructive, not least to the recipient of the money. Issues about trust and honesty must be taken into account.

- You can inform all members of the family and clearly give the reasons for your choice. While this is the most honest and open approach, it will not necessarily pre-empt accusations of favouritism. In this case, you can only reassure other family members that if an equivalent need arose, they would receive the same consideration.

- You can find a means to distribute money equally but not at the same time, or in the same way. For example, if help is being given with a mortgage, there could be a promise to help the others with their mortgage in the future. And if, when the time comes, there isn't enough money available to do this, make a promise to others that they will inherit a compensatory amount – if this is possible.

- You should be aware that monetary gifts outside the family can be resented by family members. They may feel, for whatever reason, that friends or carers are spongers, or spendthrifts, or have less of a claim to your money than they do.

- Differing treatment of siblings can fester and spill out even many years later. Expecting family members to be 'reasonable', generous or self-sacrificing is unrealistic. Try to be as transparent as possible in your dealings with family members but be aware that this isn't always recip-rocated.

- The situation may be just too complicated emotionally and financially and so if you do not want to give money away, for whatever reason, you should not feel under pressure to do so. In the end it is up to you, and you alone, how you dispose of what is yours.

- With all of the above in mind, if you haven't yet drawn up a will, now may be the time to think seriously about doing so. If there's any possibility of acrimony amongst family members after your death, it's so much better to have a lawyer deal with it within the terms of your will than have the family fight it out. And where possible, discuss how you might distribute your material possessions and sen-timental objects with family members in good time, so that there isn't a nasty dispute later about who gets the family photos or the silverware.

Money and our partners

We have probably lived with our spouse or partner long enough to have an idea how they feel about saving and spending money. As we've seen, whereas attitudes to money may be modified they won't change fundamentally with age. Now, with a more restricted budget and a limited number of years in which to spend our money, divergent views on finances and expenditure within a household can become more marked. RELATE, the relationship counselling agency, says that there is more disruption in relationships over the question of money than over any other issue.

Over the years I made good financial provision for all the family and now, at 68, feel we should use some of our savings to enjoy life while we can. I would really like to go on a world tour looking up long-lost friends on the way. But my wife Betty adamantly refuses, saying that if anything happened to me she would be left with only just enough to live on and that we should continue to economise. We've had some serious arguments about this and I've shown her all the accounts to prove to her that she's wrong. But she just says I am unrealistic and selfish. I can't decide what to do, accept her view or spread my wings.

Patrick, 68

When the person you live with spends – or saves – more than you would like, there are a number of issues to be taken into account: the source of the money, past spending patterns, your common vision of the future, the power balance in your relationship, different financial commitments and so on. When there is disagreement over how to spend money in later life, you can be pretty sure that this was an issue earlier on as well. But when you feel so insecure that you want your partner to spend less, or conversely, when you feel 'rich' enough to want to go out and spend more before it's too late, it's no consolation to know that the problem has been around for years. Instead, it's helpful to look at strategies to overcome your by-now longstanding and incompatible attitudes to money.

Here are some questions to ask yourself:

- To what extent do I really want to change the present situation? I've put up with it for so long, what has changed now?

- If I decide unilaterally to save or spend our money what will the consequences be? Am I ready to accept those consequences?

- If my partner is more responsible for looking after our money than I am, why is this? Can this situation be modified or changed in my favour? Or do I simply want my partner to change his or her spending habits?

- Should the money issue be seen in a wider context? How does my partner feel about growing older, the coming years, what does she or he hope we will do together? Can I relate to those feelings?

- If I feel we should save or spend more, can I back this up with the figures? How reliable are the figures, do they stand up to scrutiny?

- Knowing that feelings of uncertainty and insecurity, justifiable or not, are the most common reasons behind a reluctance to spend, how can I give reassurance?

- Conversely, if my partner won't agree to economise despite the evidence, what's behind this? Is it a denial of the fact we're growing older and facing some uncertainty? How can I get beyond this with my partner?

- How can we reach a compromise about long-term financial arrangements? What can we reach agreement on, and do we have the financial flexibility to maintain divergent spending habits?

- If my partner won't consider a change or a compromise, can I turn to others for help? Either financial advice or relationship counselling? Can a friend or family member talk to my partner?

Money and love

> I feel that my grandchildren are having a tough time, as they continue to be the focus of a struggle between their divorced parents. My daughter gives them pocket money and the occasional treat but is strict about unnecessary expenses. When they visit or are on the phone the children often ask me for money to go on school outings or for leisure activities. My daughter has no objection to this; she says it is between me and the children. I adore the children of course, but I'm beginning to wonder how wise it is to give them money so often. I wonder what their reaction would be if I stopped. I'd hate to be remembered only as a source of money.
>
> Frances, in her late fifties

Our immediate response to this might be 'Well, if the grandchildren's love and attention is only motivated by money, then it's not worth having.' But that reaction isn't realistic, ignoring as it does Frances's need to be with her grandchildren and her fear that if she stops the money, the grandchildren may contact her less frequently. The grandchildren may also feel, rightly or wrongly, that their grandmother is the only one they can turn to for 'treats' and may see her withdrawal as yet another adult betrayal.

Money and social relationships are so closely linked that it can be very hard to separate them. We always hope that people take us for what we are, and that by giving love, admiration and support we will receive positive feedback in return, regardless of money. But haven't most of us had a family friend or relation whom we loved to see because they always came with a small gift, or whom we enjoyed visiting because their house had such a breathtaking view of the sea?

To what extent can we disentangle the personal from the material and financial?

In Frances's case the choice involves grandchildren, but the same situation crops up in a variety of ways. If we no longer make a generous contribution to the charity fund, will we be invited to the annual dinner? If we refuse to lend an unreliable friend the money for a deposit, will it be held against us?

It's easy to feel angry or let down when we believe that the loved one or friend is more interested in what we can give them than in us. And sometimes our feelings are justified. If the phone calls stop when we cut the supply of gifts, the message is unmistakable.

Thinking it through

If you are faced with Frances's dilemma, you could ask yourself the following questions:

- Is this a financial or an ethical problem? Do I feel it's wrong to give the money as a point of principle, or because I can't really afford to?

- Can I offer something in place of the money? An outing, some interesting family memorabilia, my time and attention?

- Is the money they're expecting to receive going to be used for something that I think is reasonable?

- Does the request for money hide a need or demand for something else, such as attention or affection? If so, can I provide enough of both to make the recipient feel safe and loved, without myself feeling that I'm being taken for a ride?

- Can I give a set amount every month and say there will be no more?

- Can I defer the payment by saying that I can't help this month but will see what I can do next time?

- If I believe that the recipient 'only loves me for my money', what evidence do I have for this? Has it been borne out by their past behaviour? Or is it more a reflection of my own unease or insecurity about this relationship?

Enjoy it

The money we have and how we choose to spend it will play a large role in shaping our experience of later years. It would be wonderful if concerns about money simply disappeared, but they don't. If anything they become more acute as we recognise that the income we have for our remaining years is more or less fixed. Although we do not, as a rule, discuss personal money matters with other people except in extreme circumstances, it is a fact that the choices we face are very similar for all of us whatever our income, it is only the scale and frequency that change. It comes as a relief to know that these concerns are shared by others and that we all have to decide how best to balance security and comfort with future provision and help to others.

But rather than feeling constrained by our income, regretting what we can no longer have, we should do our best to take pleasure in whatever our money can do for us – particularly if these pleasures are small and simple. While unexpectedly large expenses or financial obligations to other people make for tricky negotiations it is our overall approach to money issues that will have the most impact. Finally, I hope this chapter has provided you with some alternative ways of viewing and tackling these complex issues successfully.

Conclusion

....

THIS BOOK IS ABOUT your choices in later life: what they are, how to make them and what the likely consequences might be. It assumes that you can, if you so wish, follow different paths at different points in your life, and that the challenge is to assess, select and then act on choices that are both wise and appropriate.

Despite the fact that we have very different backgrounds, resources and circumstances, it is still possible to draw up guidelines that are relevant to us all because everybody has the same overriding wish: to live in comfort for the rest of their lives. Not just in material comfort, although this is very important, or physical comfort – as free as possible from aches and pains – but above all, in psychological comfort.

Coming to terms with our past and who we are now, feeling at ease with and satisfied by, our relationships with friends, family and the outside world constitute the universal leitmotif of later years.

We have seen that we are faced with some serious choices, many of a practical nature and relatively easy to make, others involving those dear to us or a dramatic shift in the way we behave, which need more thought and which are harder to implement.

As a result of reading this book, you may make some choices, and hopefully well-informed ones, but unfortunately that is not enough! Choosing an option is only the first step in the process that will bring results; making the necessary moves to transform a choice into action is a further step that few of us are able to take without some misgivings.

As I have pointed out throughout this book, the secret of transforming our choices into satisfactory outcomes is, wherever possible, to do things in small, incremental stages. But between choice and action there is an intermediary step that acts as a bridge and that is *accepting change*.

Acceptance of change

You may have decided to do nothing and think that in this way you have pre-empted change and that it won't happen and things will go on as before. Unfortunately as we grow older, those changes *will* happen whether we like them or not, or whether we have accepted them or not. This is an undeniable fact of life: change happens despite us. Learning to deal with change is an important skill at any age, but becomes vital if you are to be psychologically comfortable with life over 50.

Fear of change is about loss of control, watching helplessly from the sidelines as your social and physical environment is transformed. It is clear therefore that the more you can decide things for yourself, whether it is about where to live or what medication to take, the more you are the instigator of change and exert some control over what happens to you, the greater your psychological comfort level. And not all change is for the worse.

> For 40 years we had a magnificent nut tree in our garden, which we loved and admired. It was a constant in our lives and when it began to die we were devastated. We did everything we could to keep it alive but the day came when it had to be cut down. When it was removed we felt it was the end of an era and nothing would be the same again. And of course it wasn't – but to our surprise, with this huge tree gone, our garden was full of sunlight. Other plants and flowers flourished and we found ourselves with a whole new perspective. We have photos and happy memories of our nut tree and learnt a lesson: as much as we fear change, it can often bring surprises in its wake.
>
> Marla and Carlos, in their sixties

When I set out to write this book I intended to be a non-judgemental recorder of what I learned with the sole aim of condensing and simplifying much of the confusing material and advice around us, and to share this with you, the reader, at an individual level to help you make wise and relevant choices

But as I mentioned in the Introduction, I very quickly became aware that much of the discussion concerning our age group, for whatever reason, sidestepped many important issues and that the valid concerns you raised went unaddressed. At the same time I discovered that there was a far greater commonality between us than I had first supposed.

Of course, grouping people together at the expense of their individuality and talking in generalities about people in their twenties, thirties or eighties is no more acceptable than assuming all redheads or Mancunians think and act alike. So it is perhaps only to be expected that many of you expressed reluctance at being viewed as part of a wider group, either because you felt too young or too old to fit into one of the traditional categories. I feel this is understandable but regrettable, because, as I mentioned in the Introduction we are indeed part of a recognisable but, as yet, unrecognised group. Regrettable because many of you seemed so pleased and relieved to hear that your concerns were shared by others, illustrated by the frequent comments along the lines of 'about time too', 'tell them who we really are', 'wonderful that at long last someone is taking an interest'.

From everything I have read and heard, many of you feel you are swimming against the tide, having to justify your needs and attitudes with a shared degree of annoyance, frustration or plain resignation. Annoyance, not with changes in society which infuriate many people of all ages, but with everyday irritations too insignificant to report or mention to anyone else, which highlight your perception that you are too old for this and yet too young for that. Beryl's comment sums this up: 'I was reading a magazine ostensibly for retirees and there in the middle was a full page advert for pregnancy testing! It made me realise that the editorial board of this magazine didn't have a clue!' Frustration with the ambiguity of being age-wise piggy-in-the-middle.

My conclusion is therefore that despite a frequently expressed reluctance to be part of a distinct group, this was because the groups that come to mind don't fit the image we have of ourselves. It is not customary in the UK to complain – complaining is equated with whingeing and makes us feel uncomfortable (younger people have fewer problems with this!). But does this mean we should continue to remain passive until the passage of time inevitably puts us into that more recognisable group, the over eighties?

My personal experience on the 'road to Damascus' came in a London department store. A smartly dressed lady in her sixties was staring disconsolately at the range of footwear on offer. Facing a choice of high-heeled, pointed fashion pumps or low-heeled frumpy casuals that no one at any age would select if they had any real choice, she caught my eye and said sheepishly 'There's nothing here for us is there? There never is.' She was absolutely right, but as I left the store in exasperation, it dawned on me that despite our shared frustration it didn't occur to either of us to tell the manager how we felt. We remained passive because we each thought we were the exception. Each little incident doesn't really seem to matter very much. Because we are still active and feel we have better things to do than 'make a fuss' or 'waste our breath', we keep our views to ourselves. But, it is now when we have the time, means and energy that we should be doing something to raise awareness of our concerns, to help ourselves and others, now and for the future.

Yes, there are some very active organisations out there that represent the over fifties such as Saga, and some such as Age Concern make a concerted effort to tackle discrimination, forced retirement, poorer health care for the elderly, and so on. But their energy, quite rightly, is turned principally towards helping those, mainly in old age, who cannot speak for themselves and who need their attention and resources more than we do.

So for the moment we are poorly organised, if at all, and although we are active in myriad associations that cover a huge spectrum of interests, we do not form a pressure group to express our views socially, politically or commercially.

Perhaps it is time we made our feelings known and our voices heard.

We need to raise the level of awareness; firstly by finding an acceptable name for ourselves (see page 6); secondly by constituting, joining or contacting a lobby group which aims to influence public opinion, institutions, the providers of consumer goods and services; and thirdly we could all speak up a little more on appropriate occasions to correct the stereotyping and assumptions that are so often made about us.

> In sheer frustration I decided to telephone my MP to say how I felt on issues which concern me. I do that now on a regular basis and I'm sure they are heartily sick of me on the phone, but if only others did the same maybe something would change.
>
> Gary, 62

In the meantime, to end on a gentler note, and while waiting, passively or not, for the world to catch up with us, we can look forward to the coming years, make the very best we can of them and see this time of transition as a time of opportunity.

When faced with choices remember that others have been there before you. Few choices are irrevocable and having thought through all the options available to you, and, of course, having read this book, ultimately the choice is yours. Good luck to you all!

Notes

Introduction
1. Estrine, S. and J., *Midlife: A Manual*, Vega, 2002
2. Dorothy Youngs 'A Good Age', *Guardian Weekend*, 4 June 2005
3. Thomas Heilmann, advertising executive, quoted in *The Economist*, 27 March 2004

Part 1

Introduction
1. A survey of Retirement, *The Economist*, 27 March 2004

Chapter 1
2. First World War veterans interviewed in the *Daily Telegraph*, 11 November 2005
3. McKann and Albert, 'Keep your Brain Young'
4. Olga Raz, Israeli nutritionist, 2005
5. Helsinki Public Health Department Report, Prof. Jaako Kaprio, June 2005
6. Report by Professor Martin Gibala, quoted in *The Times*, 2005
7. François de la Rochefoucauld, *Maximes*, Vantage Press, June 2005
8. Ram Dass, *Still Here*, Hodder & Stoughton, London, 2002

Chapter 2
9. Dr Maryanne Vandervelde, *Retirement for Two*, Piatkus Books, 2004

Chapter 3
10. *Good Housekeeping*, August 2004

Part 2

Chapter 4
1. Dr Martin Seligman, 'Authentic Happiness', *Time* magazine, 17 February 2003
2. Leonie Frieda, 'Happiness', *Daily Telegraph*, March 2005

Chapter 5
3. Alain de Botton, 'Anxiety', *Daily Telegraph Magazine*, 2005

Chapter 6
4. Estrine, S. and J., *Midlife: A Manual*, Vega, 2002
5. Susan Jeffers, *End the Struggle and Dance with Life*, Hodder & Stoughton, 23 May 2005
6. Jon Kabat-Zinn, *Wherever You Go, There You Are*, Piatkus Books, August 2004

Chapter 7
7. Mahler, R. and Goldman, C., *Secrets of Becoming a Late Bloomer*, Hazelden, 1995

Chapter 8
8. Dr Maryanne Vandervelde, *Retirement for Two*, Piatkus Books, 2005

Chapter 9
9. Zoe Heller, *Notes on a Scandal*, Penguin, March 2004
10. Ram Dass, *Still Here*, Hodder & Stoughton, London, 2002

Part 3

Chapter 11
1. Focus on Families, Office of National Statistics, 2005

Chapter 12
2. *The Junior Antiques Road Show*, BBC TV broadcast, 2006

Chapter 13
3. Mary Helen and Shuford Smith, *101 Secrets of a Great Retirement*, Roxbury Park Books, Lowell House, 2000

Chapter 14
4. Dr Maryanne Vandervelde, *Retirement for Two*, Piatkus Books, 2005
5. Mary Helen and Shuford Smith, *101 Secrets of a Great Retirement*, Roxbury Park Books, Lowell House, 2000

Chapter 15
6. Quoted in *The Week*, 16 September 2006

Part 4

Introduction
1. 'A Survey of Retirement', *The Economist*, 27 March 2004

Resources

Useful addresses

Age Concern
Astral House
268 London Road
London SW16 4ER
Tel. 020 8679 8000

Better Government for Older People
207–221 Pentonville Road
London N1 9UZ
Tel. 020 7843 1582

British Wheel of Yoga
25 Jermyn Street
Sleaford
Lincolnshire
NG34 7RU
Tel. 01529 306851

Caring Matters
132 Gloucester Place
London NW1 6DT
Tel. 0207 402 2702

Cruse Bereavement Care
Cruse House
126 Sheen Road
Richmond upon Thames
Surrey TW9 1UR
Tel. 020 8939 9530

The Department of Health Publications
PO Box 777
London SE1 6XH
Tel. 0800 555 777

The Grandparents' Association
Moot House
The Stow
Harlow
Essex CM20 3AG
Tel. 01279 444964

Help the Aged
207–221 Pentonville Road
London N1 9UZ
Tel. 020 7278 1114

Tai Chi Finder Ltd
21 The Avenue
London E11 2EE
Tel. 0845 8900744

MIND
Granta House
15–19 Broadway
London E15 4BQ
Tel. 020 8519 2122

The National Pensioners' Convention
9 Arkwright Road
London NW3 6AB
Tel. 020 7431 9820

The Patients Association
PO Box 935
Harrow
Middlesex HA1 3YJ
Tel. 020 8423 9111

The Pilates Foundation UK Ltd
P.O. Box 57060,
London EC4P 4XB
Tel. 07071 781 859

The Pre-retirement Association
9 Chesham Road
Guildford
Surrey GU1 3LS
Tel. 01483 301170

Saga Group
Saga Building
Middelburg Square
Folkestone
Kent
Tel. 01303 771111

Telephone Counselling Careline
Tel. 020 8514 1177

The University of the Third Age
26 Harrison Street
London WC1H 8JW
Tel. 020 7837 8838

Further reading

General

A Survival Guide to Later Life, Marion Shoard, *Daily Telegraph*, Constable and Robinson, 2004

Choosing Happiness, Stephanie Dowrick, Rider, 2005

Retirement for Two, Dr Maryanne Vandervelde, Piatkus Books, 2005

Our Bodies

100 Ways to Live to be 100, Dr Roger Henderson, Piatkus Books, August 2002

Dealing with Chronic Pain: The Pain Management Approach, J. Barrott, On Stream Publications, 1999

Dr Ruth's Sex after 50, Ruth Westheimer, Quill Driver Books, 2005

Earl Rindell's Supplement Bible, Pocket Books, 2002

Food as Medicine, Khalsa Dharma Singh, Pocket Books, 2004

For Men Only: Looking your Best, Gerald Imber, William Morrow, 1998

Great Sex after 50, Eve Capello, Dr Eve Publishing, 2000

Health Boosters, Michael Van Straten, Mitchell Beazley, 2006

How to Get First Class Medical Care: Dealing with Doctors, Hospitals, Families and Friends, Clarke and Evans, Brick Lane Press, 1998

Love after 50, Maria Eggleton, Helm, 2005

The Good Look Book: a Comprehensive Guide, John H. Hartley, Longstreet, 1992

The Power of Make-up: Looking Your Best at any Age, Trish McEvoy, Simon and Schuster, 2005

Our Minds

Alone, Alive and Well: How to Fight Loneliness and Win, Barbara Powell, Harper Collins, 1986

Cognitive Behavioural Therapy for Dummies: Common Sense Techniques for Improving Your Mind and Mood, R. Wilson and R. Branch, John Wiley and Sons Ltd, 2005

Dealing with Grief and Loss: Hope in the Midst of Pain, Serendipity, 2001

End the Struggle and Dance with Life, Susan Jeffers, Hodder & Stoughton, 2005

Finding Serenity in the Age of Anxiety, Robert Gerzon, Bantam, 1998

The Alzheimer's Prevention Plan, Patrick Holford with Shane Heaton and Deborah Colson, Piatkus Books, 2005

The Anatomy of Bereavement, Raphael, Basic Books, 1983

The Serenity Principle, J. Bailey, Harper, 2006

Towards Serenity: A Common-sense Approach, V. B. Carderelli, Author House, 2003

Wherever You Go, There You Are, Jon Kabat-Zinn, Piatkus Books, 2004

Our World

Caring for Elderly Parents, Ruth Whybrow, Crossroads Publishing Co. (US), 1996

Status Anxiety, Alain de Botton, Penguin, 2005

The Friendship Crisis: Finding, Making and Keeping Friends When You're Not a Kid Any More, Marla Paul, Rodale Books (US), 2006

The Good Granny Guide, Jane Fearley-Whitingstall, Short Books, London, 2005

The Grandparents Book: Thoroughly Modern Grandparenting, Linda B. White, Gateway Books (US), 1989

No Regrets, A 10-step Program for Living the Present and Leaving the Past Behind, H. Beazley, John Wiley and Sons, 2004

Our Money

Living on a Fixed Income, Niki Chesworth, Robinson, 2006

Money in Retirement, Jonquil Lowe, 'Which?' Guide, 2005

The Complete Guide to Personal Finance, Jeff Prestridge, Random, 2001

You and Your Money, Alvin Hall, Hodder & Stoughton, 2005

Some interesting websites

www.helptheaged.org.uk	Help the Aged
www.ageconcern.org.uk	Age Concern
www.citizensadvice.org.uk	Citizens Advice Bureau
www.u3a.org.uk	University of the Third Age
www.who.int/ageing/en	Global Movement for Active Ageing
www.helpage.org	Help Age International
www.ncvo-vol.org.uk	National Council of Voluntary Organisations
www.guardian.co.uk	Listings of Jobs in the Voluntary Sector
www.bwy.org.uk	The British Wheel of Yoga
www.pilatesfoundation.com	The PILATES foundation UK Limited
www.nhsdirect.nhs.uk	NHS Direct Online
www.grandparentsapart.co.uk	Grandparents Apart
www.taichifinder.co.uk	Tai Chi Finder Ltd

Index